BRITAIN'S PRESERVED

TRAMS

AN HISTORIC OVERVIEW

BRITAIN'S PRESERVED

TRAMS

AN HISTORIC OVERVIEW

PETER WALLER

PEN & SWORD
TRANSPORT

AN IMPRINT OF PEN & SWORD BOOKS LTD.
YORKSHIRE – PHILADELPHIA

Britain's Preserved Trams: An Historic Overview

First published in Great Britain in 2021 by
Pen and Sword Transport
An imprint of
Pen & Sword Books Ltd.
Yorkshire - Philadelphia

ISBN 978 1 52673 901 8

Typeset in 11/13 Palatino by SJmagic DESIGN SERVICES, India.

Printed and bound in India by Replika Press Pvt. Ltd.

Pen & Sword Books Ltd incorporates the Imprints of Pen & Sword Books Archaeology, Atlas, Aviation, Battleground, Discovery, Family History, History, Maritime, Military, Naval, Politics, Railways, Select, Transport, True Crime, Fiction, Frontline Books, Leo Cooper, Praetorian Press, Seaforth Publishing, Wharncliffe and White Owl.

For a complete list of Pen & Sword titles please contact

PEN & SWORD BOOKS LIMITED
47 Church Street, Barnsley, South Yorkshire, S70 2AS, England
E-mail: enquiries@pen-and-sword.co.uk
Website: www.pen-and-sword.co.uk

or

PEN AND SWORD BOOKS
1950 Lawrence Rd, Havertown, PA 19083, USA
E-mail: Uspen-and-sword@casematepublishers.com
Website: www.penandswordbooks.com

CONTENTS

Abbreviations..6

Acknowledgements...7

Introduction...8

The Trams in Service..11

Bibliography...157

ABBREVIATIONS

BEC	British Electric Car Co Ltd
EATMS	East Anglian Transport Museum Society, Carlton Colville
EMB	Electro-Mechanical Brake Co Ltd
ERTCW	Electric Railway & Tramway Carriage Works Ltd, Preston
GCR	Great Central Railway
GEC	General Electric Co
GNR(I)	Great Northern Railway (Ireland)
LCC	London County Council
LCCTT	London County Council Tramways Trust
LPTB	London Passenger Transport Board
LRTL	Light Railway Transport League
LUT	London United Tramways
M&G	Mountain & Gibson
M&T	Maley & Taunton
MET	Metropolitan Electric Tramways
NELSAM	North East, Land, Sea & Air Museums
NTM	National Tramway Museum
OMO	One Man (Person) Operation
STMS	Scottish Tramway Museum Society
TLRS	Tramway & Light Railway Society
TMS	Tramway Museum Society
TSO	Tramcar Sponsorship Organisation
UEC	United Electric Car Co Ltd
VAMBAC	Variable Automatic Multi-notch Braking & Acceleration Control

ACKNOWLEDGEMENTS

The majority of the images in this book have been drawn from the collections held by the Online Transport Archive; these include the following: Arthur Brookes, R.R. Clark, Barry Cross, C. Carter, Keith Carter, Gerald Druce, Ian Dunnet, W.S. Eades, Marcus Eavis, George Fairley, Harry Haddrill, Philip Hanson, W.G.S. Hyde, Martin Jenkins, D.W.K. Jones, R.W.A. Jones, J. Joyce, F.N.T. Lloyd-Jones, Harry Luff, John McCann, John Meredith, Struan J.T. Robertson, Hamish Stevenson, Ian Stewart, Phil Tatt, Julian Thompson, Geoffrey Tribe, F.E.J. Ward, Peter N. Williams, Ian L. Wright and W.J. Wyse (LRTA [London Area] Collection). Others come from my father's collection and as credited. The National Tramway Museum houses the negatives of W.A. Camwell, D.W.K. Jones, Maurice O'Connor, Hugh Nicol, R.B. Parr and H.B. Priestley. My thanks are due to Alan Brotchie, Simon Fozard and David Packer for the provision of certain images. As with my earlier books, I would like to express my sincere thanks to Martin Jenkins for ideas and comments on the book.

INTRODUCTION

It is now almost 100 years since the first 'preserved' tram in Britain was restored – the Aberdeen horse car returned to a near original condition from its electrified state in the early 1920s – but the number of historic trams secured during the inter-war years could be numbered on the fingers of one hand. Most pre-war tramway systems that were abandoned during the period disappeared almost without trace. Post-the Second World War, however, as the final great systems were consigned to the history books, the concept of securing trams for posterity developed.

It was an enthusiast tour of Southampton that led to the first tramcar to be preserved privately when 'Knifeboard' car No 45 was acquired. A collection during the tour followed by an appeal through the pages of *Modern Tramway* resulted in the funds being raised to purchase the tram but then a new problem arose: where to store it? Over the next decade, No 45 and a handful of other preserved trams led an itinerant – and insecure – life, reliant upon the generosity of individuals – such as C.T. Humpidge as general manager in Bradford – to provide accommodation. Not all of the trams that were preserved in these early days did survive and there were some notable losses – in Dublin and Liverpool, for example – where vandalism and nature led to once-preserved trams being scrapped. Initially much preservation was co-ordinated by the Museum Committee of the LRTL; this was, however, to morph into the Tramway Museum Society in the mid-1950s.

The key to the long-term survival of many of the newly preserved trams was to obtain secure accommodation and the purchase of land and buildings at Crich, in Derbyshire, in 1959, was to achieve this. Gradually, the trams already acquired were moved there and the timing was important in that it allowed a significant number of trams from systems then in the final stages of conversion – Leeds, Glasgow, Sheffield and Grimsby & Immingham – to be acquired in the knowledge that a permanent base was available. Over the past sixty years, the facilities of the Crich site – now the National Tramway Museum – have grown ever more impressive and the museum has become one of the most significant tramway collections in the world with a standard of vehicle restoration that is almost second to none. The scale of the museum's collection has grown, with a result that a number of vehicles now have to be stored away from the main museum site.

If the tramway preservation movement had been reliant solely on trams that had been acquired as 'withdrawn from service', the number and variety of vehicles available for posterity would be much smaller than today. A large number of bodies were sold off for second uses – often as holiday accommodation or farm buildings – and one of the great successes of the preservation movement has been the rescue and restoration of many of these trams. The first – Bradford No 104 – was retrieved from Odsal Stadium in the mid-1950s and, again with the support of C.T. Humpidge, restored to an operational condition at Thornbury Works, where it used to make occasional trips using the trolleybus overhead and still extant tram track until the mid-1960s. The first tram at Crich to undergo a resurrection was Leicester No 76; this was the pioneer for many of the superbly restored trams that are either on display or in operation at the museum.

Since Crich became operational, it has been joined by a number of other operational tramway museums – Beamish, Birkenhead (with its street running), Black Country

Museum, Carlton Colville, Seaton and Summerlee – as well as the historic cars that remain in operation in Blackpool, Douglas and Great Orme as well as the Manx Electric and Snaefell Mountain railways. In addition, there are a number of museums – such as the Riverside in Glasgow – that have static tramcars on display.

This book is not, however, about tramcar preservation; it is an examination of those tramcars that have survived to the modern day. Wherever possible, the photographs illustrate the tram that is now preserved whilst still in operation on its home system; when that is not possible, the sister cars are used to illustrate the types when still in service. Not all of the trams described have been restored; indeed, many are still little more than decayed bodies that have been rescued with a view towards restoration. Whilst many of the featured trams are open to public inspection and enjoyment, others are in storage or private ownership. Not every tram that survives is covered, but the trams featured offer a representative selection to portray how well the preserved trams of the British Isles reflect the history of the tramcar in these islands over 150 years.

In compiling the book, I decided to make certain exclusions, in particular, trams that remain in operation with or stored by their original owners. Thus, the Douglas horse trams that remain available for public service are not covered although a representative selection of those sold off and preserved are featured. This applies equally to the trams operated at Great Orme and on the Manx Electric and Snaefell Mountain railways. Given the sheer number of Blackpool trams that do survive, the decision was taken again to include a representative selection – including the most historic cars – rather than see Blackpool dominate. This means, effectively, that most of the trams held as part of the heritage fleet at Rigby Road are excluded as are the other first-generation ex-Blackpool cars that are stored there. Most of the non-Blackpool trams based at Rigby Road are, however, covered. If your favourite tram is omitted, please accept my apologies; it might be possible, in the future, to produce an enlarged and updated edition when, it is to be hoped, many more of the surviving hulks may well have been restored to their former glory!

The early years of tramcar preservation in the British Isles was not always a great success and there are a number of significant tramcars that were secured for preservation only for them to be eventually scrapped as a result of vandalism or lack of covered accommodation. Following the closure of the Dublin United Tramways system in July 1949, three trams were preserved – including 'Luxury Car' No 132 – and stored in the open. However, as can be seen in this view, the cars suffered from vandalism and all were eventually scrapped. *Marcus Eavis/Online Transport Archive*

In addition to those trams that were preserved for a period and then – for whatever reason – scrapped or otherwise disposed of, there were also many examples of operators offering trams for preservation. In 1956, following the final closure of the Dundee system, my father was offered two trams – one of the 'Lochee' cars (such as No 26 seen here at the Lochee terminus on 2 August 1952) and one of the cut-down single-deck works cars – on the proviso that they be removed from corporation property as quickly as possible. The lack of secure accommodation and the difficulty in trying to arrange this and transport meant that, unfortunately, the offer had eventually to be declined with the result that no Dundee electric tram survives. *Michael H. Waller*

Many of today's preserved trams owe their survival to a long second career after withdrawal converted into accommodation or farm buildings. These are the remains of Lanarkshire Tramways Co No 53 in a field near Beith, recorded prior to their recovery in 1986. The car, in its original guise, can be seen on page 76; three decades on, the preserved and operational tram at Summerlee shows how even derelict bodies like this can be restored to their original glory. *Ian Stewart Collection/Online Transport Archive*

THE TRAMS IN SERVICE

In 1874, the Birkenhead-based Starbuck Car & Wagon Co supplied eight single-deck horse trams to the Sheffield Tramways Co. One of these was No 15, which was based at Tinsley and allocated to the Brightside route. Although the last horse trams operated in the city on 11 November 1902, No 15 was not to be scrapped but was converted to electric traction with a Brill 21E four-wheel truck fitted for use as a works car based on Nether Edge depot. Renumbered 166, it was used to assist in the movement of trucks and partially completed trams between Nether Edge and the workshops at Tinsley. Fitted with a heavier duty truck in 1913, the car was renumbered 375 in 1933 and it is in this guise that the car is pictured here at the junction with Charlotte Road outside Queens Road Works towards the end of its second career; it was withdrawn in 1946 and the painted over 'Sheffield' allied to the white-painted collision fender show wartime modifications. On 11 July 1946, the tram appeared hauled by two horses as – spuriously – No 1 to help mark the 75th anniversary of the Sheffield system. Stored thereafter and losing its heavyweight truck in 1956, there was a possibility that the body might be scrapped; however, in the late 1950s, its remains were rescued by local members of the TMS and, using equipment from Glasgow, was fully restored. In 1961, No 15 returned to its home city where it operated briefly prior to Christmas over the still-extant track along The Moor. On 25 August 1962 it was also to operate for the first time at Crich before inaugurating the museum's first passenger service on 2 June 1963. The tram has made a number of further visits to Sheffield since then and has been used occasionally at Crich. *Maurice O'Connor/NTM*

In 1896, the Portsmouth Street Tramways Co acquired a number of horse trams that dated originally to 1880 from the North Metropolitan Tramways Co Ltd. Following the corporation's take-over of the company's assets on 1 January 1901 and the conversion of the tramway to electric operation four of the ex-North Met horse cars – Nos 70-73 – were converted to electric traction as Nos 81-84 and equipped with Brill 21E four-wheel trucks. No 84 – pictured here – was used as a rail grinder until 1919 and survived in passenger service thereafter until the final closure of the system on 10 November 1936. Preserved by the corporation, No 84 thus became the first British electric tramcar to be preserved. It has been on display at the Milestones Museum of Living History, Basingstoke, since the museum opened in 2000. *John Meredith Collection/ Online Transport Archive*

Between 21 November 1881 and 15 March 1901, the Leamington & Warwick Tramways & Omnibus Co Ltd operated a three-mile long 4ft 8½in gauge horse tramway between the two towns. A total of nine horse cars were operated, supplied by the Metropolitan Railways Carriage & Wagon Co Ltd of Saltley, Brown Marshall & Co of Birmingham and the Midland Railway Carriage & Wagon Co Ltd of Shrewsbury. Typical of the fleet was No 7 seen here; sister car No 8 was initially preserved by the Birmingham Railway Museum but was relocated to Beamish in 2012. The tram is currently under restoration and will re-emerge as Newcastle & Gosforth No 49, incorporating parts from the original of that number, when completed. *Barry Cross Collection/Online Transport Archive*

Opened on 28 June 1882, the short – just under two-mile – 3ft 0in gauge Portstewart Tramway linked the town with its railway station at Cromore. In order to operate the line, two small tram engines were acquired from the Leeds-based Kitson & Co – No 1 (Works No 56) in 1882 and No 2 (Works No T84) in 1883. In 1897, the original company went into liquidation and was acquired by the Belfast & Northern Counties Railway. The new owners invested in the line – including the purchase of a third tram engine and new passenger cars – prior to its acquisition by the Midland Railway in 1903 (as part of the Northern Counties Committee and thus it became part of the London, Midland & Scottish Railway at Grouping in 1923). This view records tram engine No 2 with a G.F. Milnes & Co-built trailer car of 1899 and a closed van. The line was closed on 30 January 1926. Engines Nos 1 and 2 survived in storage; No 1 was shipped to Hull in May 1939 and now forms part of the collection on display at Streetlife Museum of Transport, whilst No 2 remained in Northern Ireland and is now based in the Ulster Folk & Transport Museum at Cultra. *Barry Cross Collection/Online Transport Archive*

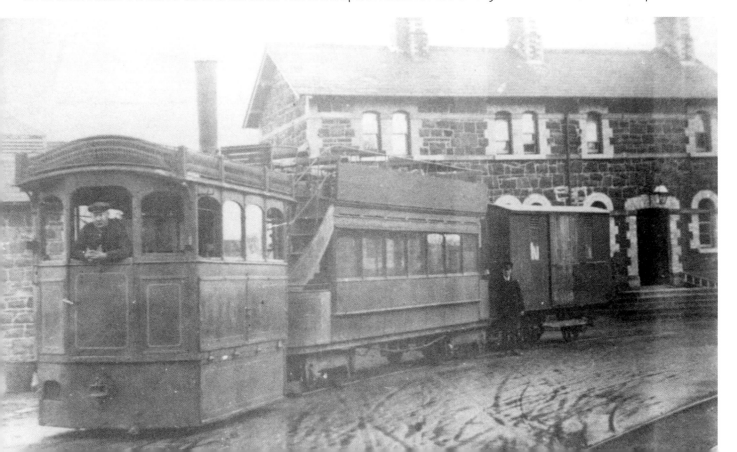

Above: **In 1877,** it was decided that the existing horse tram used on the short line from Fintona Junction to Fintona, part of the Great Northern Railway (Ireland) system, required replacement but it was not until 1883 that the new tram, built by the Birmingham-based Metropolitan Railway Carriage & Wagon Co, was delivered. Originally numbered 74 and with a mahogany finish, the car was quickly renumbered 381 in the railway's carriage stock and repainted into blue and white. A second tram – No 416 – was built in 1913 but was destroyed by fire before delivery, leaving No 381 – seen here under the station roof at Fintona – to soldier on alone until the line's final closure on 30 September 1957. Secured for preservation, No 381 is now based at the Ulster Folk & Transport Museum at Cultra. *Barry Cross Collection/Online Transport Archive*

Opposite above: **The 3ft** 0in gauge Giant's Causeway, Portrush & Bush Valley Railway & Tramway Co Ltd was one of the earliest electric tramways in the British Isles. Linking Portrush with the Giant's Causeway on the Antrim coast, the first section of the line, from Portrush to Bushmills, opened on 29 January 1883 with the section from Bushmills to the Giant's Causeway following on 1 July 1887. For the opening of the line, the Shrewsbury-based Midland Railway Carriage & Wagon Co supplied four-wheel two trailers – Nos 1 and 2 – and two power cars - Nos 3 and 4. The two power cars were converted into additional trailers by 1902. The line was originally powered by a third rail, but this was eventually replaced by overhead. Here No 2 is pictured alongside one of the crossbench power cars and one of the crossbench trailers. Both Nos 1 and 2 survived until the closure of the line in 1949 and the latter was preserved. It is now on display at the Ulster Folk & Transport Museum at Cultra. *C. Carter*

Opposite below: **The origins** of Giant's Causeway No 9 are uncertain, although restoration work has suggested that it may date towards the opening of the line in 1883. It was originally constructed as an unpowered trailer car by the Midland Railway Carriage & Wagon Co and was unusual in having two compartments – for first and third class passengers – split by a sliding door. Following the purchase of an additional Peckham four-wheel truck in 1909, No 9 was converted into a power car. This required the body to be strengthened as the original was not designed to accommodate the weight of a trolleypole. The open platforms were fully enclosed shortly thereafter. In 1945, the body of the car was refurbished using the ornate side panels from No 3 and it is in this condition that the car is pictured at the Giant's Causeway terminus on 21 September 1948. Following closure of the line on 30 September 1949, the body of No 9 was sold and used for a number of years as a café at Youghal in County Cork. The body was rescued and is currently under restoration at the National Transport Museum of Ireland at Howth. *Ian L. Wright/Online Transport Archive*

Above: **The third** tram to survive from the Giant's Causeway is trailer car No 5. This was one of three supplied by the Shrewsbury-based Midland Railway Carriage & Wagon Co in 1885. Nos 5-7 could each accommodate twenty-four seated passengers and all three survived through until the closure of the line in September 1949. Following closure, No 5 – which is pictured here outside Portrush station – was preserved and is now displayed fully restored in the Ulster Folk & Transport Museum at Cultra. *Arthur Brookes Collection/Online Transport Archive*

Opposite above: **The story** of Bessbrook & Newry No 2 – seen here towards the end of its life – is a complex one. For the opening of the 3ft 0in gauge line on 1 October 1885, the Ashbury Carriage Co of Manchester supplied two single-deck bogie cars – one was 33ft 0in in length and the other was 21ft 8in. In 1928, the company acquired Dublin & Lucan trailer No 24; regauged from 3ft 6in to 3ft 0in; the car was to become Bessbrook & Newry No 7. Withdrawn in 1942, the body from No 7 was transferred to the frames of No 2 and extended to create a new No 2. As such, it remained in service until the closure of the line on 10 January 1948. Following withdrawal, No 2 was purchased by Mather & Platt of Manchester and, having been refurbished, was used as a cricket pavilion at the company's Park Works. In 1955, the company donated the tram to Belfast Corporation for inclusion in the local transport museum; it is now on display in the Ulster Folk & Transport Museum at Cultra. *F.N.T. Lloyd-Jones/Online Transport Archive*

Opposite below: **On 29** September 1885, the first electrically-powered street tramway in England commenced operation; this was the three-mile long conduit-equipped line of the Blackpool Electric Tramway Co Ltd. For the line's opening, a total of ten cars – six open-top double-deckers and four single-deck crossbench trams – were supplied by the Starbuck Car & Wagon Co Ltd of Birkenhead and by the Lancaster Carriage & Wagon Co Ltd. The latter supplied four of the double-deck cars – Nos 3-6 – and two of the crossbench trams – Nos 9 and 10. Initially, all of the double-deck cars were equipped with four-wheel trunnion trucks but those on the Lancaster-built trams were replaced by four-wheel trucks supplied by the Wolverhampton-based Electric Construction Co Ltd in 1894. Following withdrawal in 1912, No 4 became a works car; Nos 5 and 6 were also converted into works cars (in 1919). No 4's second career was to last more than twenty years before it was taken out of service and stored; it is in this condition that the tram is pictured here in Bispham depot. For the 75th anniversary of the conduit tramway in 1960, No 4 was restored to an operational condition (retaining its trolleypole) and given the spurious fleet number 1 (which had originally been carried by one of Starbuck-built double-deckers). In this condition, it was transferred to the Museum of British Transport at Clapham in 1963 and to the TMS's Clay Cross store twelve years later. Transferred to Crich in 1979, the car was restored to as near original condition as possible – losing its trolleypole in favour of batteries for propulsion – and was based in Blackpool between 1985 and 1991. It remains on static display at the NTM. *John Meredith Collection/Online Transport Archive*

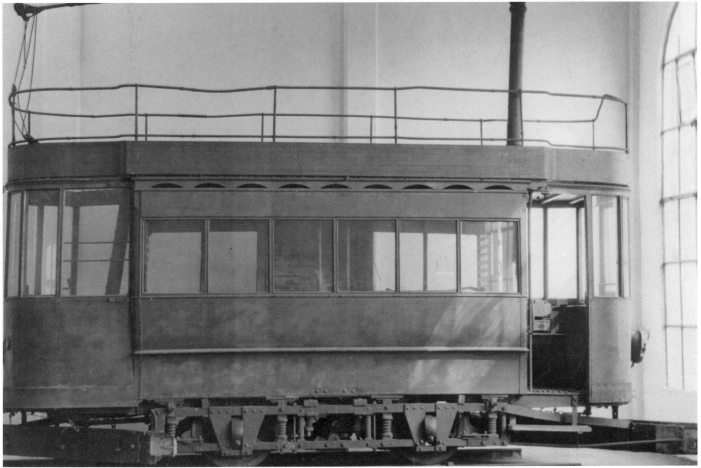

For the opening of the 3ft 6in gauge Wolverton & Stony Stratford Steam Tramway on 27 May 1887, the Shrewsbury-based Midland Railway Carriage & Wagon Co Ltd supplied four double-deck bogie trailer cars. Three of these could accommodate 100 seated passengers and the fourth could seat eighty. The original line, which extended for slightly more than 2½ miles, was extended the following year by a further two miles to Deanshanger, but the company hit financial problems and went bankrupt in 1889. It reopened as far as Stony Stratford in 1891, but the Deanshanger section was abandoned. Ownership passed to the London & North Western Railway in the early 1920s and thus to the London, Midland & Scottish Railway at Grouping in 1923. The line closed on 19 May 1926 (having last operated on 4 May 1926 as a result of the General strike). Although none of the passenger cars was preserved at the time, parts of the lower deck from two of the 100-seat cars were restored into a single car with a replica upper deck constructed from the original drawings. The restored body was fitted with replica bogies in 2001 and the vehicle is now on display at the Milton Keynes Museum. This view, taken at Wolverton station shortly before closure, sees tram engine No 2 (built by Thomas Green & Sons Ltd in 1887) with one of the 100-seat trailers. *Real Photographs/Barry Cross Collection/ Online Transport Archive*

In 1890, G.F. Milnes & Co supplied Douglas Corporation with two open toastrack cars – Nos 21 and 22 – but, in 1908, No 22 was fitted with a retractable canvas cover roof. During the 1920s, the existing roof on No 22 was replaced by a fixed one and it is in this guise that the car is pictured heading west in suitably inclement weather during the summer of 1956. No 22 was to remain in service as a passenger tram until 1976; it was then converted into a mobile shop outside the depot at Strathallan Crescent, a role that it fulfilled until 2009 when it was transferred to the Jurby transport Museum, where it remains on display. Note the four corner lights on the roof; these were designed to permit the operation of the tram at night. Unmodified No 21 remains part of the operational fleet. *Phil Tatt/ Online Transport Archive*

Prior to the take-over of the company-operated routes in Glasgow on 1 July 1893, the North Metropolitan Tramways constructed four sample open-top double-deck horse trams – Nos 542-45 – for the corporation. Thereafter, a further 359 horse trams were supplied between 1894 and 1897 prior to the rapid conversion of the existing system to electric operation; in order to supplement the new electric trams 120 of the existing horse-car fleet were converted to electric operation. The last horse trams operated in the city in 1902 and No 543 – which is seen here in store during 1947 (prior to being damaged in the Newlands depot fire of April 1948) – was retained in original condition. It was restored in 1922 to help mark the Golden Jubilee of the first tram operation in the city and was also to feature in the closure procession held in September 1962. Preserved, the tram was initially displayed at Coplawhill works and then Kelvingrove but is now housed within the city's Riverside Museum. *Hugh Nicol/NTM*

Steam trams commenced operation in Dundee, courtesy of the Dundee & District Tramway Co, on 20 June 1885. A total of thirteen steam engines, Nos 1-13, were supplied to the company by Thomas Green & Son Ltd of Leeds between 1885 and 1894; the last of these is seen here with one of the company's double-deck trailer cars. Following the cessation of steam tram operation by Dundee Corporation, which had taken over the company's assets on 1 June 1899, on 14 May 1902, all of the thirteen steam tram trailers acquired were disposed of. The lower saloon of No 21, which had been built by G.F. Milnes & Co of Birkenhead in 1894, became a fishermen's hut at Crombie reservoir, to the north-east of the city, where it survived for more than sixty years. Rescued in 1969 and initially under restoration in the open at Blackpool, the body was also stored for a time at Clay Cross, prior to a move to Bolton where its restoration was finally completed using similar Milnes plate bogies to those on which it originally operated but acquired from an ex-Douglas Corporation cable tram. Although it has never operated at Crich, the tram is on display at the museum.
Dr Struan J.T. Robertson Collection/Online Transport Archive

For the opening of the Douglas South Electric Tramway – later the Douglas Head Marine Drive Co Ltd – on 2 September 1896, Brush supplied a batch of open-top double-deck 'toast track' cars fitted with American-built Lord Baltimore No 2 four-wheel trucks. The 4½-mile long line – the only standard gauge tramway or railway on the Isle of Man – was eventually operated by eight power cars and eight trailers. Operation of the tramway was suspended during the First World War and again from 28 August 1939; it was never to re-open. The tramway's assets were sold to the Isle of Man Highways Board post-war and the track and overhead removed between 1946 and 1948. This left the tramcars isolated in their depot at Little Ness until 1951, when all bar No 1 – seen here Port Soderick pre-war – were scrapped. During 1951, members of the LRTL visited the line's depot before the fleet was disposed of and decided to try and ensure that one of the cars was preserved. Fortunately, the efforts of one member of the LRTL, Keith Pearson, persuaded the Highways Board to remove the tram – no easy feat from a remote location – and, in 1955, the tram was transferred to the Museum of British Transport at Clapham. Based there until 1964, when Clapham closed, No 1 then passed to the Science Museum; loaned to the TMS in March 1975, ownership of the car passed to the NTM in May 1997. Conserved in full working order – albeit unlikely to operate in public service due to its historic condition (it is the oldest surviving tram in original condition, never even having been rewired in its 125-year history) – the tram remains on static display at Crich. *Real Photographs/Barry Cross Collection/Online Transport Archive*

The 3ft 0in gauge Upper Douglas cable tramway, constructed and operated by the Isle of Man Tramways & Electric Power Co, linked the Clock Tower and Broadway via Victoria Street and Prospect Hill. The line opened on 15 August 1896, but the section from York Road to Broadway was not to last long, being closed for safety concerns over the gradient. The remaining section passed to Douglas Corporation in 1902 and was abandoned on 19 August 1929. A total of fifteen trams were acquired to operate the route, eight of which – Nos 71-78 – came from G.F. Milnes & Co in 1896. No 73 is pictured here at the junction of Woodbourne Road and York Road. Following closure, Nos 72 and 73 were sold, with their bogies, to be converted into a bungalow at Jurby. The two were rescued for preservation in 1968 and, between 1973 and 1976, the best parts were used to construct one restored tram (which has No 72 at one end and No 73 at the other). The tram is now on display at the Jurby Transport Museum. *Barry Cross Collection/Online Transport Archive*

Recorded at the Derby Castle terminus of the Douglas horse tramway on 26 August are Nos 38, 35 and 37. The latter two were from a batch of six open crossbench cars – Nos 32-37 – that was supplied by G.F. Milnes & Co in 1896. Over a sixty-year period – from 1908 to 1968 – the cars were modified by the addition of bulkheads. Of the six, only two – Nos 32 and 36 – remain part of the operational fleet whilst No 35, sold in 2011, is now displayed at the Home of Rest for Old Horses, Richmond Hill. The remaining three cars were sold at auction in August 2016. No 33 was sold privately for £1,200, No 34 was sold for £1,300 and was converted into a motorised road vehicle in 2018 (now based at the Jurby Transport Museum), and No 37 was sold for £1,100 privately; Nos 33 and 37 also remain on the Isle of Man. *John Meredith/Online Transport Archive*

Above: **In order** to supplement its existing fleet of electric trams, Aberdeen Corporation converted a number of older horse trams between 1900 and 1902. In all, thirteen open-top trams were electrified using Brill 21E four-wheel trucks and Westinghouse electrical equipment and motors; Nos 57-65 had long canopies whilst Nos 66-69 had short ones. One of the latter is recorded here, prior to about 1909 (in about that year Nos 66-69 were converted to snowploughs and salt cars), turning into Union Street from Holburn Street with the tracks towards Queens Cross, to the west, heading along Alford Place to the right. The last ex-horse cars were all withdrawn during the five years after the end of the First World War. Following withdrawal, one of the Nos 57-65 batch – either No 61 or 63 – was preserved in 1924 and restored as a horse tram – as delivered in 1896 (save for retaining its Brill truck). *Michael H. Waller Collection*

Opposite: **The restored** Aberdeen horse tram – allocated fleet number 1 (although whether it actually bore that number as a horse car is uncertain) – is seen here in Mannofield depot on 1 April 1950 looking in a somewhat careworn condition. *Modern Tramway*, in its report on the final Aberdeen abandonment in May 1958 (with No 1 leading the final closure procession), noted the rapidity with which the surviving trams were scrapped and commented, 'The horse tram will, however, be kept for the time being in the hope that it can be presented to a museum, if there are any takers.' Fortunately, a new home for the tram – Shrubhill Works in Edinburgh alongside preserved Edinburgh No 35 – was found and the tram was transferred there in 1959. Edinburgh was to be its home until 1982, when it returned to Aberdeen and is now normally on display in the Grampian Transport Museum. *Michael H. Waller*

Above: **The decision** of Glasgow Corporation to take over the operations of the Glasgow Tramways & Omnibus Co following the expiry of the company's lease and to electrify the network resulted, in 1897, in the construction of No 665. This was a single-deck car with offset entrances, built at Coplawhill, with bogies supplied by the Metropolitan Carriage & Wagon Co. Based on this prototype – albeit now with central entrances – a further twenty cars – No 666-85 – were constructed in 1898. The same manufacturer supplied the bogies. Nicknamed the 'Room & Kitchen' cars, the type was not successful, with the corporation opting to construct – in large numbers – the 'Standard' four-wheel type. As a result, the single-deck cars had short lives. No 672 – seen here in an official photograph after withdrawal in August 1907 – was modified to become part of the corporation's fleet of works trams as Mains Testing No 3. As such, it remained in service until October 1953. Stored thereafter, following pressure from the STMS, the car was restored to near original condition between 1959 and 1962 and was to feature in the closure procession for Glasgow's tramcars in September 1962. Preserved thereafter, the car is now on display in the Riverside Museum, Glasgow. *GCT official/Ian Stewart Collection/Online Transport Archive*

Opposite: **For the** opening of the Blackpool & Fleetwood Tramroad Co on 14 July 1898, G.F. Milnes & Co supplied ten crossbench single-deck cars – Nos 1-10 – and three similar trailers – Nos 11-13; all were fitted with bogies supplied by Milnes, with Nos 11-13 being motorised in about 1905. A further three crossbench cars – Nos 25-27 – were delivered from Milnes in 1898 with the final three of the type – Nos 35-37 – coming from UEC in 1910. All passed to Blackpool Corporation following its acquisition of the company's assets on 1 January 1920, with the trams subsequently being renumbered. Nos 1-10 became corporation Nos 126-35. The modernisation of the Blackpool fleet in the 1930s saw the crossbench cars withdrawn but a number were to have a second career as works cars. This included No 127 – ex-Blackpool & Fleetwood No 2 – which was used as a snowplough after 1940, having been withdrawn two years earlier. The car survived in this guise until the 1950s and, with the forthcoming 75th anniversary of the tramway planned for 1960, it was one of the cars selected for restoration to mark that event. Restored to its original livery, the tram is pictured here at Fleetwood with another of the trams restored – 'Dreadnought' No 59 – and one of the 'Balloon' cars of the 1930s in late 1960. Ownership of the tram was transferred to the TMS and the car moved to Crich in September 1963. No 2 was the first tram to operate under the museum's new overhead – on 6 June 1964 – and also the first electric tram in public service (on the following 5 July). Since then, No 2 has returned to Blackpool for further anniversaries but remains based at the NTM; it is currently on display but requires a major overhaul before it can return to service. *W.G.S. Hyde/Online Transport Archive*

When the Great North of Scotland Railway opened its branch line from Ellon to Boddam, on the Aberdeenshire coast on 2 August 1897, the station at Cruden Bay was more than a quarter of a mile from the railway-owned hotel. In order to connect the two, the railway constructed a 3ft 6in gauge tramway, which opened on 1 June 1899. For the service, the railway constructed two small single-deck tramcars in its workshops at Kittybewster; numbered 1 and 2, the trams were fitted with Peckham Cantilever Type 7B four-wheel trucks and were originally painted in a livery of purple lake and cream. Passenger services on both the Boddam branch and the Cruden Bay tramway ceased on 31 October 1932, although the tramway continued in operation for the movement of supplies to the hotel. The tramway last operated on 31 December 1940, with the hotel having been requisitioned for the army. Neither the hotel nor the tramway reopened post-war. The two trams – seen here towards the end of their lives in London & North Eastern Railway ownership and in the varnished teak livery that they wore latterly – were sold for use as summerhouses. The bodies of both were recovered in 1988 and used in the reconstruction of a single preserved car; this is now on display at the Grampian Transport Museum, Alford. *Real Photographs/Barry Cross Collection/Online Transport Archive*

The Chesterfield & District Tramways Co was empowered in 1879 to construct four route miles of horse tramway serving the town; in the event only the two miles from the centre to Brampton were completed with services commencing on 8 November 1882. This company failed and, from 1886, services were operated by the Chesterfield Tramways Co until the corporation took over on 22 November 1897. In 1899, the corporation supplemented the small fleet that it inherited with two new single-deck trams – Nos 7 and 8 – that were supplied at £125 each by G.F. Milnes & Co of Birkenhead. However, the new trams were destined for a short working life, as horse tram operation in Chesterfield ceased on 22 December 1904. The body of No 8 – seen here during its short career in the town – was sold for use as a summer house. Rescued in 1934, the tram was restored by Chesterfield Corporation's transport department. Initially restored to the maroon and primrose livery of the electric trams – as demonstrated by Chesterfield No 7 at the NTM – No 8 was displayed in Nottingham in 1947 before being later transferred to the British Transport Commission for display at the Museum of British Transport. Returning to its home town, it was again restored – this time to its original Prussian blue and Primrose livery – before a brief transfer to Crich in 1982. In 1985, No 8 returned to the NTM on permanent loan from the Science Museum; ownership was formally transferred to the NTM in 2016. The tram remains in the museum on display in a restored but non-operational condition; it last ran in 1993. *Barry Cross Collection/Online Transport Archive*

Above: **Between 1899** and 1904, Sheffield Corporation put into service sixty-nine single-deck cars supplied by five different manufacturers to deal with routes with low railway bridges and those with steep gradients. Of these, Nos 39-52 and 187-92 were built by G.F. Milnes & Co. With the exception of Nos 39-52, which were originally equipped with Peckham Cantilever 10A four-wheel trucks, all were fitted with Brill 21E four-wheel trucks. As originally built, these cars were equipped with open vestibules and five-window bodies. By the end of the First World War, the single-deck cars were becoming obsolete and thirty-five were sold to other operators between 1918 and 1920; of the remainder, twenty-one were rebuilt as double-deckers (during 1906 and 1907 or between 1915 and 1918) and nine were converted into snowploughs between 1913 and 1921. The remaining four passenger cars were all withdrawn by the end of 1921. No 46 was converted into a snowplough in 1921 and was to survive in this guise until 1950. As part of the work involved in this conversion, the body was shortened by one bay whilst the vestibules were enclosed in 1940. The tram was renumbered 97 in 1924 and 275 in 1926; it assumed its final identity – No 354 – in 1937. Retained for preservation, the tram was restored as No 46 – albeit in a condition that it had never operated in whilst carrying that number (and on a Brill 21E truck, which it had acquired in 1937) – in 1958 before being used in the final closure procession in October 1960 as it was the oldest extant Sheffield electric tram. It is in this condition that the tram is pictured here. Transferred to Crich later that month, the car was used in service until 1973; since 2005, the car has been in store, although the NTM has plans for its full restoration. *George Fairley Collection/Online Transport Archive*

Opposite: **The story** of the evolution of the Glasgow 'Standard' four-wheel car is long and complex; second only in numbers to the 'E/1' class of the London County Council, more than 1,000 of the type were built between 1898 and 1923. Initially built as open-top and with open-lower deck vestibules, the type gradually evolved so that latterly they all operated as fully-enclosed, with many of the cars passing through various phases of development. There is not the space here to examine the type in detail – readers seeking a fuller explanation of the development of the 'Standards' are recommended to read the detailed account in Ian Stewart's excellent *The Glasgow Tramcar* (1983) – but a number of the type have been preserved in various conditions. The oldest of the type in preservation is No 779; this was completed at Coplawhill Works on a Brill 21E four-wheel truck in April 1900. About a decade later, the tram was fitted with an open-balcony top cover; it was to remain in this condition until it was rebuilt as fully enclosed in November 1930. Surviving in service until December 1959, it was to appear in the closure procession in September 1962 having been restored to its 1910 condition; it is now based in the Riverside Museum in this state. On 30 October 1959, the car is seen in Albert Drive, Coplawhill, with a service on route 3 towards Mosspark. *Hamish Stevenson/Online Transport Archive*

The second oldest Glasgow 'Standard' to survive in preservation is No 812. This was completed at Coplawhill in May 1900, which is pictured here operating on a route 14 service; this route – which linked Cross Stobs with Arden – was converted to bus operation on 29 September 1956. No 812 was initially completed as an open-top car. An open-balcony top cover was fitted in about 1910 and subsequently the lower deck vestibules were enclosed. The car was rebuilt as fully enclosed in September 1930. At the same time, it was equipped with a longer wheelbase – 8ft 0in – 21E-type truck and its trolleypole was replaced by a Fischer bow collector (equipment on which Glasgow standardised until the final conversion of the system in September 1962). These improvements enabled the top speed of the car to be increased from 23mph to 32mph. As a result of the Suez crisis of 1956, which led to a brief delay to the conversion programme (trams did not rely on diesel, which was in scarce supply as a result of the Anglo-French invasion of the Canal Zone), No 812 had an unplannd overhaul, which led to its survival for longer than perhaps anticipated. It was finally withdrawn during the summer of 1960; it was to move to Crich in August the same year. Unlike No 22 (see page 96), No 812 has been preserved in its post 1930 condition and has operated at Crich in more than 40 operating seasons. At the time of writing, it is out of service awaiting an overhaul. *R.F. Mack*

In late 1900, Sunderland Corporation took delivery of six open-top cars – Nos 13-18 – supplied by ER&TCW on Brill 22E bogies; however, these cars were not an immediate success and, early the following year, they were converted to four-wheel cars on Brill 21E trucks. All six were rebuilt as fully enclosed between 1920 and 1922, at which stage they received replacement Brill Radiax four-wheel trucks; these were again replaced during the early 1930s, when No 13 received a M&T swing-link truck, Nos 14-16 and 18 Peckham P22s (although No 16 operated for a period with a Peckham P35) and No 17 an English Electric swing-link truck. With the post-war contraction of the Sunderland system, all were withdrawn by the end of 1953, with the exception of No 13, which survived into January the following year. The lower saloon of No 16 – seen here operating on the Circle route (a service that was converted to bus operation on 3 January 1954) – was sold for use at a football ground and then reused on a farm; it was rescued for preservation in 1989 and fully restored to its final fully-enclosed condition in 2003. It is based at Beamish. *D.W.K. Jones/NTM*

Above and opposite: **Between 1899** and 1904 Sheffield Corporation acquired 172 open-top uncanopied cars, including two that were rebuilt from horse trams. Of these, 30 – Nos 59-88 – were supplied by ERTCW on Brill 21E four-wheel trucks in 1900. All 172 were fitted with top overs between 1903 and 1913, the vast majority – 126 in all – being equipped with short covers such as that carried by No 78 seen here in 1912. In 1922, Gateshead & District acquired eight of these cars, including one of the ERTCW-built batch – No 74 – which were all rebuilt between December 1925 and June 1926 with platform canopies, lower-deck vestibules and revised open-balcony top covers. The exact sequence of the renumbered cars in Gateshead is uncertain but, following the final closure of the Gateshead system in 1951, the lower saloon of Gateshead No 33 – pictured at the Museum on 4 March 1950 – was sold for use as a garden shed. This was acquired for preservation and moved to Crich in September 1990. There the tram was restored as Sheffield No 74 incorporating parts from the similar short top covers rescued in 1970 from Nos 215 and 220 along with an ex-Leeds Peckham Cantilever truck. The restoration – part funded by the Tramcar Sponsorship Organisation and by the Science Museum – was completed in 1995. The recreated No 74 is not the original car restored but an amalgam that reflects a stage – otherwise not covered in the museum's collection – of British tramcar design. *Barry Cross Collection/Online Transport Archive /John Meredith/Online Transport Archive*

A further Glasgow 'Standard' preserved in No 585, which is now based in the Science Museum store at Wroughton. This car was originally constructed at Coplawhill in May 1901 and was fitted, like No 779, with an open-balcony top cover in about 1910. It emerged as a fully enclosed car in September 1930 and it is in this guise that the tram was recorded on 3 July 1958 at the Mount Florida terminus of route 12 to Paisley Road Toll. Withdrawn in June 1961 (although used on a tour in October 1961), the tram was privately preserved by Alex Brown later that year with the owner intending it to join other trams at the Middleton Railway in Leeds. Fortunately, this plan was not pursued, and it was donated to the Science Museum; it left Glasgow for its new home in November 1962. Cosmetically repainted to its 1930s condition with blue route colour, the tram was displayed at the Science Museum until the late 1990s when, as part of a major revamp of the museum's exhibition space, it was transferred to Wroughton. *Hamish Stevenson/Online Transport Archive*

Prior to the opening of the Stockport Corporation system on 26 August 1901, ERTCW supplied six open-top cars – Nos 1-6 – of the initial batch of ten that were fitted with Brill 21E four-wheel trucks. These trams were used to test the new system and for driver training. In total, ERTCW supplied thirty similar cars – Nos 1-30 between 1901 and 1903. No 5, which is seen here at Hyde Town Hall in July 1929, was fitted with an open-balcony Brush-built top cover in 1921 and was equipped with enclosed lower-deck vestibules in 1939. As such, the car was to survive in service until 1948. Following withdrawal, the body of the car was sold for use as a summerhouse until rescued for preservation in 1969. Following restoration to operational condition, in its original open-top and unvestibuled state using a second-hand truck acquired from Oporto, the car has been based at Heaton Park since the summer of 2011. *Hugh Nicol/NTM*

For the opening of the Great Northern Railway (Ireland)'s Hill of Howth tramway – from Sutton to the Summit on 17 June 1901 and thence to Howth on 1 August 1901 – Brush supplied eight open-top trams – Nos 1-8 – on Brill 22E maximum-traction bogies. Although constructed with windscreens, the offside of each vestibule was originally left open; these were subsequently enclosed. In the 1930s, the livery of grained mahogany, which had replaced the original crimson lake and ivory in 1912, was itself supplanted by blue and cream; this revised scheme was retained until the final closure of the tramway on 31 May 1959. Two of the eight cars – Nos 5 and 8 – were withdrawn and cannibalised for spares in 1958 but the remaining six cars survived until final closure. Although No 3 was preserved, this car was – along with Nos 9 and 11 – left in the open and was scrapped following vandalism. No 2, seen here alongside No 8 at the Summit, was more fortunate. Following the line's closure on 31 May 1959, it was purchased for preservation and shipped across the Atlantic. It remains on static display in Perris, California. *J. Joyce Collection/Online Transport Archive*

Above: **A second** of the original batch of Hill of Howth cars to survive is No 4, which is seen here at the Barren Hill loop; it is now on display at the Ulster Folk & Transport Museum at Cultra. *R.W.A. Jones/Online Transport Archive*

Opposite above: **The Gateshead** & District Tramways Co, a subsidiary of BET, ordered forty-five new trams for the introduction of its electric services on 8 May 1901. Of these, ten, Nos 1-10, were single-deck combination cars supplied by ERTCW on Brill 21E four-wheel trucks. In February 1916, No 7 was seriously damaged in an accident on Bensham Road Bank and, when it re-entered service in 1920, it had been rebuilt with an eight-window body. In 1938, the car was renumbered 52, having received a replacement 8ft 0in wheelbase track in place of its original 6ft 0in unit, and, as such, remained in service until 1951, when it was the last four-wheel single-deck tram in service on any British tramway. It is seen here post-war retaining its white-painted collision fender; the photograph predates the 1950s as the tram received a basic repaint in that year, which lacked the lining out visible in this view. Privately preserved, with the 6ft 0in wheelbase truck from No 45A, by William Southern, a motorman with the company, the tram spent some years in his garden before relocation to Crich in May 1960 – one of the earliest trams to arrive there but never operated. Although there were plans to restore it, efforts went instead on putting Gateshead No 5 and Newcastle No 102 back into service and, in 1970, No 52 was transferred to the TMS store at Clay Cross. Unfortunately, it was to suffer serious fire damage in 1999 as a result of an arson attack but, following approval by the TMS membership, the car was transferred to Beamish in January 2014. It is the museum's plan eventually to restore the damaged car. *R.R. Clark/Online Transport Archive*

Opposite below: **In 1901** Brush supplied Aberdeen Corporation with a batch of twelve open-top short-canopy cars fitted with Brill 21E four-wheel trucks. Originally numbered in a different sequence to the first eight cars, these twelve were soon renumbered 9-20. From 1904 onwards, the cars were fitted with longer canopies and open-balcony top covers. No 15 was so equipped in 1906 and is pictured here in that condition. In 1912 it was fitted with folding windscreens to a design patented by the then Aberdeen general manager, R.S. Pilcher, who subsequently became general manager at Edinburgh and then Manchester. No 15 was withdrawn in 1930 and its body was moved to Loirston for conversion into a house. Rescued in 2013, the body was based at the Dundee Transport Museum, in the former Maryfield tram depot, from August that year to January 2019, when it was transferred to the Grampian Transport Museum. Owned by the Aberdeen & District Preservation Trust, No 15 is currently under restoration at Alford. *George Fairley Collection/Online Transport Archive*

In 1901, the Midland Railway Carriage & Wagon Co Ltd supplied Blackpool with fifteen open-top trams – Nos 27-41 – fitted with the same supplier's four-wheel trucks. These were the 'Marton Box Cars'. Of these, fourteen received replacement four-wheel trucks between 1906 and 1911, including No 31 that received an M&G Radial truck in either 1906 or 1907. Twelve of the batch received open-balcony top covers between 1910 and 1914. A further modification saw five of the type – Nos 27 and 29-32 – converted to bogie cars using Hurst Nelson maximum-traction bogies reused from trams in the Nos 42-53 series. Nos 30 and 31 reverted to open-top condition at about the same time, although both received new open-balcony top covers in 1928. It is in this condition that No 31 is pictured at North Pier in about 1934; the view must post-date mid-1933 as the view also records one of the streamlined 'Railcoaches' introduced that year and pre-date September 1934 when No 31 was withdrawn. Alongside No 31 is one of the Lytham St Annes fleet. *D.W.K. Jones Collection/Online Transport Archive*

Following withdrawal in September 1934, No 31 became a works car – No 4 – in March 1935. Pictured here on Redbank Road, Bispham, in August 1951, the modifications that the car underwent for operation as an overhead line car – enclosed lower-deck vestibules and a tower in place of its open-balcony top cover – are evident. Renumbered 754 in March 1972, the tram was used as a test-bed for the operation of pantographs during 1974 and 1975. Withdrawn in April 1983, the car was preserved at Beamish where it was restored to the condition – open-top and open-vestibule – in which it operated between 1920 and 1928, regaining its original fleet number. Still based at Beamish, the car returned to its home town for a year between March 2016 and March 2017. *Phil Tatt/Online Transport Archive*

A total of eighty-one open-top uncanopied cars – Nos 107-87 – were supplied by Brush to Manchester Corporation in 1901. Originally fitted with Peckham Cantilever trucks, these were eventually replaced by Brill 21E four-wheel trucks. Typical of the batch when new is No 160, pictured here passing the Hippodrome on Oxford Road. The vast majority of the batch were fitted with open-balcony top covers before the outbreak of the First World War and a handful were rebuilt as fully enclosed during the early 1920s. The first of the type was withdrawn in the early 1920s and all had been taken out of service by the end of 1938. No 173, which had been equipped with a balcony top in about 1910, was withdrawn in 1931. Its lower deck was converted into a garden shed. Rescued for preservation initially at the Greater Manchester Museum of Transport and subsequently at the Heaton Park Tramway, No 173 is under restoration to its original open-top and uncanopied condition albeit on a Brill 21E truck. *D.W.K. Jones Collection/Online Transport Archive*

Above: **During 1901** and 1902, Bolton Corporation took delivery of twenty-two open-top cars – Nos 60-82 – constructed by ERTCW on Brill 22E bogies. All were equipped with open-balcony top covers by the outbreak of the Second World War and were further rebuilt with fully-enclosed top covers during 1929 and 1930. A number were withdrawn before the war but those that remained in service in 1940 – Nos 60/65-68/74/76-80 – were renumbered 360 etc; all these survivors were withdrawn by the date of Bolton's final conversion – 29 March 1947. One of those that did not survive to be renumbered was No 73, pictured here in its final condition with fully-enclosed top cover but open lower-deck platforms. Sister car No 66 of 1901 – No 366 after 1940 – was withdrawn in 1946 and its lower deck sold off. After some years as a summer house then a chicken hut, the remains were recovered in 1963. Under the aegis of the Bolton 66 Group, the tram was restored with a reconstructed upper deck along with controllers from Liverpool and Brill 22E bogies from Germany. Work was completed in July 1981 and the restored tram has been based at Blackpool since then, now forming part of the heritage fleet based at Rigby Road. *H.B. Priestley/National Tramway Museum*

Opposite above: **In 1902,** the GNR(I) supplemented the existing fleet on the Hill of Howth tramway through the purchase of two more open-top double-deck cars – Nos 9 and 10 – from G.F. Milnes & Co. These were originally summer only cars and, when delivered, were fitted with wire mesh rather than glazing in the lower-deck windows; this was, however, soon replaced. Nos 9 and 10 were larger than the original eight cars, accommodating seventy-three seated passengers, and were fitted with Peckham 14D5 maximum-traction bogies. During the First World War, as a result of problems obtaining paint, the company adopted a grained mahogany livery for its fleet; although Nos 1-8 lost this livery in the 1930s, Nos 9 and 10 retained it until the system's closure. Used less intensively until 1958 (their length and lack of cross springs between the bogies made them more prone to derailment), when they were modified with cross-springs reused from the withdrawn Nos 5 and 8, both 9 and 10 survived until March 1959. No 9 – seen here at Bailey Post Office – was preserved locally. Stored in the open with Nos 3 and 11 (the works car), all three suffered serious damage from vandals; although Nos 3 and 11 were scrapped, the remains of No 9 were rescued and the fully restored tram is now on display at the National Transport Museum of Ireland at Howth. *R.W.A. Jones/Online Transport Archive*

Opposite below: **No 10** – seen here in Sutton depot during August 1955 – was one of two new cars acquired by the GNR(I) for the Howth route in 1902. No 10 was acquired after the system closed on 31 March 1959 by the TMS and the car arrived at Crich in January 1960. As a result of its unusual gauge – it was built to the standard Irish gauge of 5ft 3in – it was not possible to operate the car and, as a result, it was stored at Clay Cross from May 1971 until February 1985 when it was transferred to Bolton for an overhaul. The work at Bolton included regauging the car to 4ft 8½in to permit its operation at Blackpool during the centenary of that system's opening later in 1985. The tram remained in Blackpool until November 1989 when it returned to Crich. It has not operated subsequently at the NTM but remains on display at the time of writing. *Phil Tatt/Online Transport Archive*

Opposite: **Alongside the** passenger cars acquired from Hull Corporation in 1942 and 1945, Leeds Corporation also bought the latter's single-deck works car, No 96, which entered service in Leeds in July 1945. The car was new in 1901 and was one of a batch – Nos 91-100 – supplied by Hurst Nelson on Brill 21E four-wheel trucks; converted to single-deck in 1933, No 96 was then employed as a snowplough through until the final conversion of the Hull system on 30 June 1945. Renumbered 6 by Leeds (having been retyred from Hull's centre flanges to conventional flanges), the car was used primarily as a snow plough until February 1949 and then as a stores car until rail grinding equipment was installed in 1954. It is pictured here in the Sovereign Street Permanent Way Yard; surviving until the closure of the system, No 6 was the last tram to run through the streets of Leeds when it was towed from the PW Yard to Swinegate on 8 December 1959. Preserved, the car is now based on the Heaton Park Tramway in Manchester, having been restored to accommodate passengers albeit still in single-deck form. *J. Joyce/Online Transport Archive*

Costing £1,094 when new in June 1901, the Dublin United Tramways Directors' Car was never allocated a fleet number; built at Spa Road Works, it was initially equipped with a Peckham four-wheel truck but this was replaced by one manufactured at Spa Road in 1909. Lavishly equipped – it had twelve armchairs on the lower deck, for example – the car survived through until the final closure of the Dublin system in July 1949, although it had effectively been stored from the late-1930s onwards. Acquired in 1950 by Mr H. Porter for £75, the body of the car – pictured here towards the end of its life – was moved to Dalkey for conversion into a summer house. Although suffering severe damage from a fire caused by vandalism in 1984, the remains of the car were acquired by the Transport Museum Society of Ireland in 1988 and transferred to Howth. The body is currently in store with a view to future restoration. *D.W.K. Jones Collection/Online Transport Archive*

Above: **For the** opening of the Birkenhead Corporation system on 4 February 1901, G.F. Milnes & Co supplied two batches of trams: Nos 1-13 were single-deck cars equipped with Peckham 14D3 maximum-traction bogies whilst Nos 14-44 were open-top double-deck cars fitted with Peckham Cantilever 9A four-wheel trucks. A number of the double-deck cars – including No 20 seen here in original condition – were fitted with Brush-built 'Bellamy' top covers between 1910 and 1913. The final Birkenhead trams operated on 17 July 1937 and the fleet was disposed of. The lower deck of No 20 was sold and became a fishermen's shelter at Farndon, in Cheshire, from where it was rescued for preservation by the Merseyside Tramway Preservation Society in April 1983. After being based in a number of locations, it was transferred to Taylor Street, Birkenhead – now the home of the Wirral Transport Museum – where it was restored to its original open-top condition using a Brill 21E truck acquired from Spain and controllers from Oporto. The car is operational and in use on the Heritage Wirral Tramway. *Martin Jenkins Collection/Online Transport Archive*

Opposite above and below: **During 1901,** Hurst Nelson supplied a batch of twenty uncanopied open-top cars – Nos 111-30 – on Brill 21E four-wheel trucks to Newcastle Corporation. These cars were modified between 1905 and 1907 by the addition of platform canopies and open-balcony top covers. In the early 1930s, Nos 111/15/20/21/27/30 were fitted with enclosed lower-deck vestibules as illustrated in this view of No 120 on Neville Street (this car was renumbered 24 in the late 1940s). These six cars remained in service with Newcastle Corporation until at least 1947. However, the fourteen unmodified cars were withdrawn before the Second World War and, in 1941, were sold to Sheffield Corporation where, rebuilt as fully enclosed, they re-entered service as Nos 311-24 in 1941. Their appearance in Sheffield is illustrated by No 313 – ex- Newcastle 113 – pictured in Fitzalan Square. The ex-Newcastle cars were all withdrawn during 1950 and 1951. The lower decks of two of these cars have survived. Newcastle No 114 (ex-Sheffield No 317) has been restored to original open-top and uncanopied condition at Beamish using a truck from an ex-Oporto car whilst No 117 (ex-Sheffield No 316) was rescued in 2019 by the Living ironstone Museum at Cottesmore where the intention is currently to restore it as a single-deck passenger carriage on a six-wheel underframe. *Barry Cross Collection/Online Transport Archive/C. Carter*

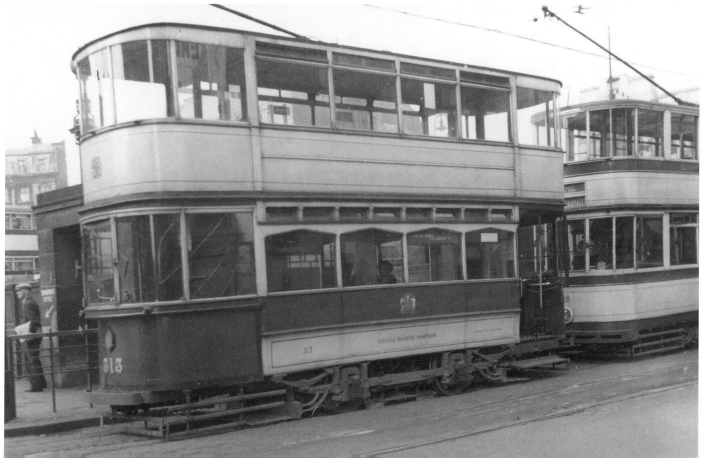

The early electric trams delivered to Nottingham Corporation came from two sources: ERTCW and G.F. Milnes & Co. The last cars supplied by the former were sixteen open-top cars – Nos 90-105 – that were delivered in 1902 on Brill 21E four-wheel trucks. All were fitted with open-balcony top covers by the outbreak of the First World War and it is in this condition that No 100 is seen in Bulwell on 3 June 1915. Sister car No 92, which had a replacement Brush lower saloon body fitted in 1923, was withdrawn in 1934 and sold to a caravan park at Torksey. The body was rescued in 1985 by the Nottingham Industrial Museum but was transferred to the NTM's Clay Cross store in October 1996 where it remains in an unrestored condition. It is regarded as future long-term restoration project. *Barry Cross Collection/Online Transport Archive*

***Opposite above*: In 1902,** following the expansion of its network, LUT purchased 150 open-top cars of Class W; of these Nos 151-211 and 237-300 were constructed by G.F. Milnes & Co at Hadley Castle in Shropshire whilst Nos 212-36 were supplied by BEC. All were fitted with Brill 22E bogies. Here Nos 159 and 284 are pictured at the Hampton Court are seen in their original condition. Of the two, No 294 was of the batch to be equipped with a top cover; of these, forty-three were eventually to pass to the LPTB, as Class U, becoming Nos 2358-402. They survived in service until the conversion of routes 57 and 67 to trolleybus operation on 27 October 1935. No 159, however, was one of forty-three cars that were scrapped or disposed of during the early 1920s at Fulwell depot. The body of No 159 was moved to Ewhurst Green, in Surrey, for use as a bungalow; it was rescued for preservation in 1978, with work on its restoration commencing at Crich in 2005, with work being largely funded by the LCCTT and TSO. The fully restored tram was launched in July 2012 and the car remains part of the NTM's operational fleet. *Barry Cross Collection/Online Transport Archive*

***Opposite below*: Cardiff Corporation** possessed only a single numbered works car; this was No 131, which was constructed by ERTCW on a Brill 21E four-wheel truck in 1902. Built as a water car-cum-track cleaner, the car was initially open and unnumbered – it only carried the number 131 between 1905 and 1926 – the body of the tram was fully enclosed in 1913. Over the years, the car's duties extended to railgrinding, storage and snowploughing until May 1949 when it was last recorded in use. The car is seen here in Adam Street on 18 May 1948. Surviving until the end of the Cardiff system on 19 February 1950, it was acquired for preservation following an enquiry by a small group of local enthusiasts (including Ian Wright and Bob Jones) to purchase it and a passenger car (No 88); all of the latter had, unfortunately, already been sold for scrap. Presented to the Museum Committee of the LRTL, No 131 was stored in a number of locations before transfer to Crich in May 1959 – the first tram to arrive at the newly-acquired site following its purchase by the TMS. Now the only water car in preservation, the tram has been fully restored and is part of the NTM's operational fleet, being used inter alia for the maintenance of the line. Apart from Crich, No 131 has also been seen at both Beamish and Blackpool over the past decade. *Ian L. Wright/Online Transport Archive*

Above: **In order** to cater for the large numbers of passengers who made use of the trams along the Promenade, the Blackpool Conduit Tramway adopted the unique 'Dreadnought' type with its twin staircases on both platforms, to a design patented by a Mr Shrewsbury. Nos 16 and 17 were built by the Midland Railway Carriage & Wagon Co Ltd in 1898. A further eighteen of the type – Nos 17-26 and 54-61 – were constructed in two batches, again being built by the Midland company. The first ten were delivered in 1900 with the second batch following in 1902. All were initially fitted with bogies also supplied by Midland. Come the 1930s, and the modernisation programme instituted by Walter Luff, and the 'Dreadnoughts' were withdrawn; one – No 59 (seen here on the traverser at Rigby Road on 6 July 1935 – the year of its withdrawal) – was retained and used for works duties, including as a mess room in Copse Road depot. The tram was restored to near-1922 condition for the 75th anniversary of the tramway in 1960 and remained in this condition until presented to the TMS in 1965. It returned to Blackpool in late 1975 for overhaul prior to town's centenary the following year and remained there until a move back to Crich in 1990. It was on static display at the museum until 1995 when it was transferred to store where, at the time of writing, it remains. *Hugh Nicol/National Tramway Museum*

Opposite above: **In 1902,** Douglas Corporation acquired a further three open toastrack cars; Nos 38-40 were supplied by G.F. Milnes & Co. The three cars were lengthened in 1934 and it is in this form that No 39 is pictured here at Summer Hill on 23 August 1995. In August 2016, two of the cars – Nos 39 and 40 – were put up for auction with the third being retained as part of the much-reduced operational fleet. No 39 was acquired by the Manx Electric Railway Society for £1,800. It and No 40 both remain on the island. *John Meredith/Online Transport Archive*

Opposite below: **Between 1903** and 1905, Newcastle Corporation rebuilt a batch of twenty-two open-top bogies cars – Nos 89-110 – on Brill 27G equal-wheel bogies. These cars had originally been built by Hurst Nelson two years earlier as open-sided end-loading single-deck cars. As rebuilt, all of the batch survived in service until after the Second World War with the exception of No 98, which had been destroyed by fire in 1917. As the Newcastle system was converted after the war, the twenty-one survivors were withdrawn between 1946 and 1949. No 102, which had been rebuilt in 1903 (and is seen here in Northumberland Street relatively soon thereafter), was withdrawn in February 1949 and was acquired by the Museum Committee of the LRTL – the forerunner of the Tramway Museum Society – two years later; it was one of the earliest trams acquired by the committee and, as a result of a lack of a permanent museum site, spent the next twenty years leading a somewhat peripatetic existence. Between 1958 and 1967, it was displayed at the National Motor Museum at Beaulieu; it reached the TMS store at Clay Cross in early 1970 and Crich five years later having been restored to 1933 condition. *John Meredith Collection/Online Transport Archive*

The evolution of tramcar design in Southampton was governed by the low Bargate through which, until it was bypassed in the 1930s, trams passed. As a result, the corporation operated for longer than many tramways open-top cars and a significant number survived into the post-war years. In 1903, Hurst Nelson supplied a batch of twelve open-top four wheel-cars – Nos 38-49 – on Brill 21E trucks. These were initially supplied in uncanopied form but five – Nos 38, 41, 42, 44 and 49 – were modified with platform canopies during 1914 and 1915. The batch also originally had only three windows per side but were modified to four windows to improve strength; the date of this work is uncertain but in most cases predates the First World War. Of the batch, all bar Nos 39, 40, 46 and 47 – withdrawn between 1919 and 1922 – survived into the post-Second World War era, although all were withdrawn by the end of 1948. No 38 – pictured here with a service towards Shirley either during or immediately after the war (judging from the white-painted collision fender) – was withdrawn in May 1948 and its body was sold off. Used as a holiday home at Fordingbridge for some years, the tram's body was recovered in 1979 and restoration commenced with the tram being provided with a new underframe and a suitable 21E truck from Oporto. With work concentrated on No 11 – see page 98 – restoration of No 38 has been deferred. *Barry Cross Collection/Online Transport Archive*

Another of the batch of twelve cars delivered to Southampton Corporation by Hurst Nelson in 1903 was No 45 – seen here in the workshops at Portswood on 1 June 1946 – which was unique amongst the batch in being fitted, between 1917 and 1929, with a short top cover with reversed stairs for use as a front-exit car. Rebuilt in 1929 back to a more original open-top condition – albeit now fitted with platform canopies similar to No 38 – to permit operation through the Bargate, No 48 was withdrawn in 1948. In August 1948, the LRTL organised a tour of the Southampton system; during this tour, which used car No 44 (in place of the scheduled No 37), participants decided to attempt to purchase the tram on which they had been riding. When making the offer, it was pointed out that No 45 was in better condition and so the purchase of this tram – for £10 (part-funded by the participants and partly by an appeal in *Modern Tramway*) – was agreed. As a result, No 45 became the first tram in Britain to be preserved privately; for the next twelve years – until moved to Crich in October 1960 – the car was stored or displayed at a number of locations, including Beaulieu and Blackpool. Restored to an operational condition, No 45 remains on display at Crich, having been last operated in service during 2015. *Ian L. Wright/Online Transport Archive*

Above: **The Glasgow** 'Standard' that has had arguably the most interesting career in preservation is No 488. Completed at Coplawhill in September 1903, it also received an open-balcony top cover in about 1910 before being further modified to fully-enclosed in December 1929. Seen here at the Burnside terminus of route 18 on 19 June 1949, No 488 was finally withdrawn in June 1961; the tram had been overhauled the previous year following a request from AMTUIR (Association du Musée des Transports Urbains, Interurbains et Ruraux) – the French museum of urban transport. No 488 was another car briefly returned to service following the Dalmarnock depot fire of March 1961 and was the last tram to operate on route 18 to and from Burnside on 3 June 1961. The tram was the first Glasgow car to cross the English Channel when it made the trip to the French capital. Some fifty years later, the tram was donated to the EATMS and was transferred to the Ffestiniog Railway's Boston Lodge Works in March (lower deck) and April (upper deck) 2013 for restoration prior to transfer to the Carlton Colville site. At the time of writing, work on restoring No 488 is awaiting completion. *Michael H. Waller*

Opposite above: **The LCC** Class B cars, Nos 102-201, were built by the ERTCW in 1903 and were designed for routes that were either lightly trafficked or had steep gradients. Initially all open-top and fitted with Brill 21E four-wheel trucks, a number were modified from 1906 onwards with open-balcony top covers until fully-enclosed top covers were adopted; those that had been fitted with open-balcony covers were also to receive enclosed balconies in due course. The 'B' class was not wholly successful and, in 1915, the process of disposal commenced. Almost sixty of the type were sold to other operators between January 1917 and April 1918; normal passenger service for the surviving cars ceased in the mid-1920s. In 1927, twenty-one of the stored cars were converted into snowbrooms, having been cut down to single-deck form. One of these was No 106 which became snowbroom No 022; the tram is pictured here in this condition in Abbey Wood depot on 17 June 1950. This car had been fitted with an open-balcony top cover in about 1908 – at which time it was also converted from reverse to normal staircases – and received a fully-enclosed top deck in 1913. Surviving until 1952 as one of the system's last works cars, No 022 was selected by London Transport for preservation with a view to restoration to its original condition; however, it was to spend the next two decades in store before presentation to the LCCTT. Restoration at the trust's Bonwell Street depot took some twelve years before the completed tram was formally presented to the TMS on 15 May 1983. Having undergone a full overhaul between 2013 and 2015, the car remains part of the NTM's operational fleet. *John Meredith/Online Transport Archive*

Opposite below: **For the** opening of the 3ft 6in gauge Chester Corporation system on 6 April 1903, G.F. Milnes & Co supplied 12 open-top cars on Brill 21E four-wheel trucks. No 3 is illustrated here heading east along Eastgate Street towards the Eastgate itself. Following the system's closure on 15 February 1930, the body of sister car No 4 was acquired by the late Harry Dibdin and stored for many years in his garden. Believed scrapped, the remains were rediscovered in 2005 and are now under restoration by the Hooton Park Trust. *Barry Cross Collection/Online Transport Archive*

Above: **The extensive** system operated by Glasgow Corporation required a significant number of works cars; some of these were converted from withdrawn passenger cars whilst others were constructed specifically for the purpose. One of the latter was Welders' Tool Van No 21 – seen here in the yard at Barrland Street Permanent Way Yard – which was built at Coplawhill in December 1903. Resembling half of a 'Room & Kitchen' car – see No 672 on p23 – No 1, as the car was originally numbered (until the early 1920s), was fitted with platform vestibules in 1939 and was to receive a replacement Brill 21E four-wheel truck, new motors and controllers in 1949. Withdrawn shortly before the final closure of the system, the tram was purchased by the TMS in October 1962 and moved to Crich. Never operated at the museum, the car has fulfilled a number of static roles – including being a temporary bookshop and on display at Wakebridge – prior to relocation to the store at Clay Cross, where it remains at the time of writing in an unrestored and relatively poor condition. *R.W.A. Jones/Online Transport Archive*

Opposite: **In late** 1903, City of Hull Tramways took a delivery of fifteen four-wheel open-top cars supplied by G.F. Milnes & Co on Brill 21E trucks; Nos 102-16 took the numbers of fifteen of the twenty-five trailer cars that had been supplied to the corporation in 1898 and 1899. The new cars were designed for operation on the new route to Hedon and, before entering into service from December 1903 through to May 1904, were fitted with Magrini adjustable top covers. These collapsible roofs were designed to be removable so that, during the summer months, the cars could operate in open-top form. These temporary top covers were replaced by permanent top covers in 1907 and, between 1920 and 1931, all of the batch, along with numerous other Hull cars, were rebuilt as fully enclosed. In the 1970s, the lower deck from one of these cars was discovered and transferred to the TMS's Clay Cross store. Unfortunately, the fleet number is unknown, but it probably survived in service until the end of the Hull system in 1945 before being sold for scrap. It survived more than a quarter of a century as a beach hut. Originally considered a long-term restoration project to plug a gap in the NTM collection, the discovery – and restoration – of Sheffield No 74 made these plans unnecessary. The body remains with the NTM in an unrestored condition. Typical of the batch is No 106 – one of the batch not sold to Leeds Corporation – which is pictured at Holderness Road on 25 February 1925 in its intermediate condition. *Barry Cross Collection/Online Transport Archive*

Above: **For the** opening of Ipswich Corporation's tramway system in 1903, Brush supplied a batch of twenty-six 3ft 6in gauge open-top trams on the same manufacturer's 21E four-wheel trucks. The following year, the same manufacturer supplied a further batch of ten cars – Nos 27-36 – which were to prove the last new trams acquired by the corporation. Following experimentation, the corporation decided to adopt trolleybuses for tramcar replacement with the first route being converted on 17 July 1925. The last trams operated on 26 July 1926 with six cars seeing further service in Scarborough and the lower deck on No 34 being used on the tramway along Felixstowe Pier. The remaining 29 trams were disposed of locally. In 1976, the body of No 33 – seen here in Corn Hill – was rescued for preservation and, following the acquisition of a suitable truck from Lisbon in Portugal in 1994, restoration at the Ipswich Transport Museum commenced in 2003. Work was completed in 2012 and the car remains on static display in the museum. *Barry Cross Collection/Online Transport Archive*

Opposite above: **Between 4** April 1903 and 31 March 1927, the Wrexham & District Electric Tramways Ltd operated a small – about 4½ route miles – network in Wrexham. To operate the 3ft 6in gauge system, the company acquired ten open-top cars supplied by Brush on the same manufacturer's A-type four-wheel trucks in 1903. A quartet from the fleet is pictured here inside the company's Johnstown depot. The lower decks of two of the fleet – believed to be Nos 4 and 6 – have, however, survived (just) and are currently stored in the open at the large exhibits store of Wrexham County Borough Museum at Bersham Colliery, Rhostyllen. *D.W.K. Jones Collection/Online Transport Archive*

Opposite below: **Running initially** from Cosham to Horndean – a distance of some six miles – the 4ft 7¾in Portsdown & Horndean, which was owned by the Hampshire Light Railways (Electric) Co Ltd (itself a subsidiary of the Provincial Tramways Co), commenced operation on 2 March 1903 with a fleet of thirteen open top trams supplied by BEC on the same manufacturer's SB60 four-wheel trucks. From 1927, the company's services were extended into Portsmouth itself over corporation-owned track but the conversion of the Portsmouth system to trolleybus operation – a process completed on 10 November 1936 – meant that the company's operations were curtailed and were converted to bus operation on 9 January 1935. Following the conversion, the fleet, which had grown significantly through the transfer of seven trams from the associated Gosport & Fareham Co in 1930, was disposed of. In 1977, the lower deck of two bodies – those from Nos 8 and 13 – were salvaged for preservation; the latter is seen here at Cosham. No 8's body is now the waiting room as part of Mills Wood station on the Old Kiln Light Railway, Farnham, whilst that of No 13 is under restoration in Portchester having been equipped with a replica SB60 truck. *Barry Cross Collection/Online Transport Archive*

Above and opposite above: **Edinburgh possessed** the largest cable tram network in the British Isles. At its maximum extent, following the conversion of the Craiglockhart route in 1907, the Edinburgh & District Tramways Co Ltd operated cable trams over some 25½ route miles. On 1 July 1919, the corporation took over and progressively converted the cable network to electric traction with the last cable cars operating on 23 June 1923. Amongst the cable cars operated were a batch of twenty – No 209-28 – uncanopied four-wheel cars that were built by ERTCW in 1903; all were equipped with short top cover in 1907 and it is in this condition that No 227 is pictured. Following the corporation take-over, a large number of the cable cars – including Nos 209-28 – were converted to electric traction mainly on Peckham four-wheel trucks. A number were later rebuilt as fully enclosed as evinced in this view of No 225 heading towards Joppa. Sister car No 226 was electrified in 1923 when fitted with a replacement open-balcony top over supplied by McHardy & Elliott. It was rebuilt as fully enclosed in 1932. Following withdrawal in April 1938, the lower deck of No 226 was converted into a holiday home before being rescued for preservation. Currently under restoration into its original cable condition. No 226 is now owned by National Museums Scotland. *Barry Cross Collection/Online Transport Archive (both)*

Opposite below: **In 1903,** Lowestoft Corporation acquired four single-deck combination cars – Nos 21-24 – from G.F. Milnes & Co that were fitted, as illustrated in this maker's view, with the same supplier's maximum traction trucks. A total of thirty-eight passengers were accommodated on transverse seating in the enclosed central compartment with a further six in each of the open smoking compartments. The only bogie trams to operate on any tramway in East Anglia, the quartet was primarily designed for operation in the winter months – although occasionally being seen during the summer as well – and all survived until the closure of the Lowestoft system on 8 May 1931. Following the conversion, the bodies of the tramcars were disposed of; one of the single-deck cars – one of Nos 21-23 – ended up being used as accommodation in the garden of a bungalow locally. Rescued in January 1990, the grounded body of the tram is now used as a small museum at the East Anglian Transport Museum at Carlton Colville. *Barry Cross Collection/Online Transport Archive*

Above: **For the** opening of the Derby Corporation system on 27 July 1904, Brush supplied a batch of twenty-five open-top four-wheel cars on the same manufacturer's AA four-wheel trucks. No 1 – seen here at the Burton Road terminus in original condition – reached the corporation's Abingdon Street depot in December 1903 and was used initially for testing the new electric equipment and crew training. Like the majority of the 4ft 0in-gauge batch, No 1 was later reequipped a with Brill 21E truck. It was also fitted in 1928 with lower-deck vestibules and an open-balcony top cover. Withdrawn in September 1933, the lower deck of the tram was sold off for use as a summer house at Mickleover. Rescued by the Derby Tramway Group in 1962 and originally based at Peartree, near Nottingham, where restoration commenced using a standard gauge UEC 21E truck (acquired from Blackpool where it had previously been used beneath the *Gondola* illuminated car), the restored car was acquired by the TMS in 1970. Since 1991, the tram has been on static display at Crich. *Barry Cross Collection/Online Transport Archive*

Opposite: **For the** opening of the Paisley District Tramways Co on 13 June 1904 British Electric Car Company Ltd supplied thirty-eight open-top cars on Brush AA four-wheel trucks. No 1-38 were all to pass to Glasgow – as Nos 1001-38 – on 1 August 1923 following the corporation's purchase of the company's assets and operations. During 1924 and 1925, sixteen cars from this batch – Nos 1009-16/18/19/22-24/27/37/38 – were converted to single-deck for use on the lightly trafficked Clydebank to Duntocher route. The unconverted cars were progressively withdrawn during the 1930s, as were four of the cut-down cars (Nos 1010/14/37/38), leaving the remaining twelve as survivors through the Second World War and into the early post-war years. The decision to convert the Duntocher route – made effective on 3 December 1949 – rendered these cars redundant and all were withdrawn or scrapped between May 1949 and March 1950. The body of No 1016 – see here at the Duntocher terminus – survived, however, and was acquired in the mid-1980s for preservation by the Scottish International Tramway Association. Based for a period at the Glasgow Bus Museum at Bridgeton Garage, the body, plus an ex-Lisbon truck acquired for its restoration, were transferred to Rigby Road, Blackpool, in January 2017, for restoration as part of the Blackpool Heritage Trust fleet. *Hugh Nicol/NTM*

Above: **For the** opening of Leicester Corporation's electric system on 18 May 1904, ER&TCW supplied a total of 100 trams; of these, 99 were open-top four-wheel cars fitted with Brill 21E four-wheel trucks whilst No 100 was a works car. All of the passenger cars were fitted with open-balcony top covers between 1912 and 1927 and, with the exception of Nos 12, 24, 29 and 44, were all rebuilt as fully enclosed between 1924 and 1937. The bulk of the Leicester system survived the Second World War, although the process of converting the system to bus operation recommenced in early 1945. No 31, seen here is its final condition, was withdrawn in March 1949, contemporaneously with the conversion of the Clarendon Park and Blackbird Road routes, and its body was moved to Markfield, in Leicestershire, for use as a farm building. It was secured for preservation in 2009 and equipped with a new steel underframe eight years later. The car is currently under restoration in its home city by the Tram 31 Project. *Barry Cross Collection/Online Transport Archive*

Opposite: **Another of** the BEC-supplied cars to the Paisley District Tramways Co in 1904 was No 17, which became Glasgow Corporation No 1017 on 1 August 1923. Another of the batch converted to single-deck form – in January 1925 – but with narrow platform doors and with most of the internal bulkheads removed, No 1017 was thereafter used as a School Car for training motormen. It was fitted with a bow collector in 1933 and was to survive on these duties, based at Langside depot, for many years and then Coplawhill. It was normally to be found in operation on the single-track section of Coplaw Street, which was unused by normal services. It is pictured in August 1960; following closure of the driving school, it was occasionally used as a works car until the system's final closure. The tram's body was sold to Ian Cormack and placed in his garden where it was used to house meetings of the STMS. It was rescued from a garden in Cambuslang for restoration in 1991; its original truck was preserved at the time and used in the restoration of Leicester No 76 (see page 66). The tram, restored to its single-deck Glasgow condition, is now operational again at the Summerlee Museum of Scottish Industrial Life. *Hamish Stevenson/Online Transport Archive*

A second ex-Leicester tram from the original batch to survive is No 76; this was one of the cars withdrawn as a result of the conversion of the Fosse Road route on 17 July 1947. Following withdrawal, its body was sold for use as a cricket pavilion at East Cowick (near Goole), from where it was rescued in August 1960. The restoration of the tram – the first at Crich to feature the resurrection of a derelict body – was completed in 1969 and utilised the Brush AA four-wheel truck salvaged from Glasgow No 1017 (see page 65). Used briefly in passenger service at Crich, No 76 is now displayed in the museum's exhibition hall. *H.B. Priestley/NTM*

Between 23 December 1904 and 23 May 1927, Chesterfield Corporation operated a small – just over 3½ route miles – system. For the opening of the system, Brush supplied twelve open-top cars fitted with the same manufacturer's Conaty four-wheel trucks. Of these, No 8 was destroyed by in a depot fire in October 1916 and was replaced by a new car; this and Nos 6, 7, 9, 11 and 12 were all fitted with open-balcony top covers during 1919 and 1920. No 7, which was slightly damaged in the 1916 fire, received its top cover in January 1919 and is pictured here in Stephenson Place. Surviving until the closure of the system, the body of No 7 was sold after closure with the two decks finding a new home as a holiday bungalow slightly to the north of Matlock. There, despite various vicissitudes, the body was to survive until being rescued for preservation in 1973. Restoration of the tram commenced in 1993 and used parts from a number of other tram bodies, including sister car No 9, before being launched on 17 May 1997. Fitted with a Peckham P22, No 7 remains part of the NTM's operational fleet. *Barry Cross Collection/Online Transport Archive*

Extending at its maximum to just over four route miles, the 3ft 6in gauge tramways operated by Lowestoft Corporation between 22 July 1903 and 8 May 1931 employed a fleet of nineteen passenger cars. Of these, fifteen were open-top four-wheel cars supplied by G.F. Milnes & Co; Nos 1-13 were delivered in 1903 and Nos 14 and 15 the following year. Following withdrawal in May 1931, No 14 – pictured here – was converted into a summer house at Gunton. Its body was rescued in the spring of 1962 by the East Anglian Transport Museum Society and transferred to Carlton Colville; fitted with an incorrect standard gauge Milnes Girder four-wheel truck from Sheffield works car No 375 and a static exhibit for a number of years, work is currently in hand to make the car operational again. *R.F. Rew/Barry Cross Collection/ Online Transport Archive*

In 1904, MET took delivery of a batch of sixty open-top uncanopied double-deck cars supplied by Brush on the same manufacturer's reversed BB maximum-traction bogies. Classified Type A and numbered 71-130, all were fitted with covered top covers during 1928 and 1929. Of the sixty built, fifty-five passed to the LPTB in July 1933 but all had been withdrawn, as the tram to trolleybus conversion programme progressed, by the end of 1936. MET No 94 – seen here at the Acton terminus of route 66 – became LPTB No 2455; withdrawn in 1935, the tram's body was subsequently used as a garden shed at Waltham Cross. Acquired for preservation, the body was transferred to the Eastbourne depot of Modern Electric Tramways with a view to full restoration. However, this did not proceed, and ownership passed to Modern Electric Tramways. In 1968, the remains of the upper deck were removed and the tram was transferred to Seaton where, with the lower deck narrowed to reflect the 2ft 9in gauge used at Seaton, the body was used to create single-deck car No 16. The restored tram was formally launched on 2 June 1994 by Larry Grayson. *D.W.K. Jones Collection/Online Transport Archive*

Another of the purpose-built works cars of Glasgow Corporation was Cable Laying Car No 1, which is seen here in early 1960. The car, which was new in 1905 and fitted with a Brill 21E four-wheel truck, was designed to accommodate huge cable drums for the purpose of installing or removing cabling. A unique vehicle, it survived in service until the end of the system in September 1962, although not used extensively after assisting in laying the cables for the city's new trolleybus system in 1949. Sold in October 1962, it was stored near Aberdeen until 1965, before being transferred to Crich. It has been stored away from the NTM since 1982 and now lacks its motors; these were transferred to Leicester No 76 during the restoration of that car. Two other works cars – Nos 10 (ex-Paisley No 50) and 22 – were also sold to the TMS in October 1962 but were always destined for scrapping to provide parts. *Hamish Stevenson/Online Transport Archive*

***Above*: Following its** acquisition of 170 open-top four-wheel cars from Brush for the inauguration of its electric system, Belfast Corporation decided to convert a number of the existing horse trams into electric cars in 1905. Initially, five were planned but such was the condition of the original bodies, when work commenced that it was decided to rebuild fifty in all; these became Nos 201-50. Fitted with Brill 21E four-wheel trucks, the rebuilt trams were outwardly very similar to the Brush-built cars (although they were slightly smaller and had quarter rather than half-turn staircases) and initially lacked platform canopies. Over the years, the type underwent some modification with the majority being fitted with both platform canopies and open-balcony top covers. One of the final survivors was No 249 – seen here on the shed fan on Gaffikin Street on 6 June 1953 – which had been converted into a snowplough five years earlier; this was one of the cars that, although equipped with canopies, never received a top cover. Following the system's closure in 1954, the already withdrawn No 249 was preserved and can now been seen at the Ulster Folk & Transport Museum at Cultra. *R.J.S. Wiseman*

***Opposite above*: For the** opening in 1904 of the 3ft 6in gauge tramways network operated by Northampton Corporation, ERTCW supplied twenty open-top trams – Nos 1-20 – fitted with Brill 21E four-wheel trucks. The following year, the same supplier delivered two further largely identical trams – Nos 21 and 22 – except that this pair was fitted with direct, rather than reverse, stairs. The latter is illustrated here in original condition on Drapery, about to use one of the crossovers on the street prior to heading north with a service to Kingsthorpe. Nos 21 and 22 (both in 1926), along with five of the earlier batch, were equipped with open-balcony top covers. The last Northampton trams operated on 15 December 1934 and the surviving cars were disposed of. There is photographic evidence of the partially dismantled trams – including No 21 – outside the depot on St James's Road prior to their removal. The lower deck of No 21 was rescued and is now in private ownership at Walton-on-the-Naze. *Barry Cross Collection/Online Transport Archive*

***Opposite below*: In 1906,** the Hastings & District Electric Tramways Co Ltd acquired a batch of twenty 3ft 6in gauge open-top cars – Nos 41-60 – from UEC; these were fitted with Brill 21E four-wheel trucks and equipped with the Dolter stud equipment for use on the sea front section. The section along the sea front used the Dolter stud method of current supply from 12 January 1907 until 26 March 1914, when operation of this section was undertaken by petrol-electric cars with the result that most – or all – of the ex-Dolter stud-fitted cars were equipped with petrol-electric motors supplied by Tilling-Stevens to operate this section. This was itself replaced by conventional overhead in 1921. This view of No 48 dates from when the tram was virtually brand-new – the original postcard is franked 3 October 1907 – when, equipped with both a trolleypole and Dolter stud equipment, it heads towards West Marina. The last Hastings trams operated on 15 May 1929. The body of No 48 – along with sister car No 56 – were rescued in March 1993, having both been used as bungalows at Camber, and both are currently under restoration at Robertsbridge, where they have been located since 2001. *D.W.K. Jones Collection/Online Transport Archive*

Between 1905 and 1931, Exeter Corporation operated a 3ft 6in gauge system that extended just under five route miles at its maximum. In all, the corporation acquired thirty-eight open-top electric trams, including a batch of six – Nos 16-21 – supplied by UEC in 1906. Like the majority of the Exeter fleet, these were all equipped with Brill 21E four-wheel trucks. The body of No 19 – seen here at St David's station in 1926, three years before it was renumbered 21 – was discovered in use as a summerhouse at Rewe in 1984. Donated to the Seaton Tramway a decade later, the lower deck was restored as single-deck car – appropriately numbered 19 – in the Seaton fleet. The rebuilt car was formally launched into service in 1998 by the then Mayor of Exeter. *J.H. Meredith Collection/Online Transport Archive*

Birmingham Corporation acquired a batch of 150 trams – Nos 71-220 – from UEC between August 1906 and March 1907; fitted with M&G Radial four-wheel trucks, these became known as the 'Radial' class. Originally ordered as open-top, changed regulations enabled the corporation to amend the order and the cars were delivered fitted with open-balcony top covers. By 1928, all of the batch had received replacement trucks – the majority receiving Peckham P35s – but the pre-war conversion programme saw all of the batch withdrawn by September 1939. However, twenty-two had not been scrapped and these were retained during the Second World War in case they were required to replace trams destroyed by enemy action. In the event, none was returned to service and they were sold for scrap in June 1945. Typical of the type was No 134, seen here at Alum Rock on a route 8 service; the lower deck of sister car No 107, which was withdrawn in September 1939, was sold off as a summerhouse at Bromsgrove. Rescued by as Aston Manor Road Transport Museum in March 1988, the vehicle is undergoing a long-term restoration programme and is now based at Aldridge. *Barry Cross Collection/Online Transport Archive*

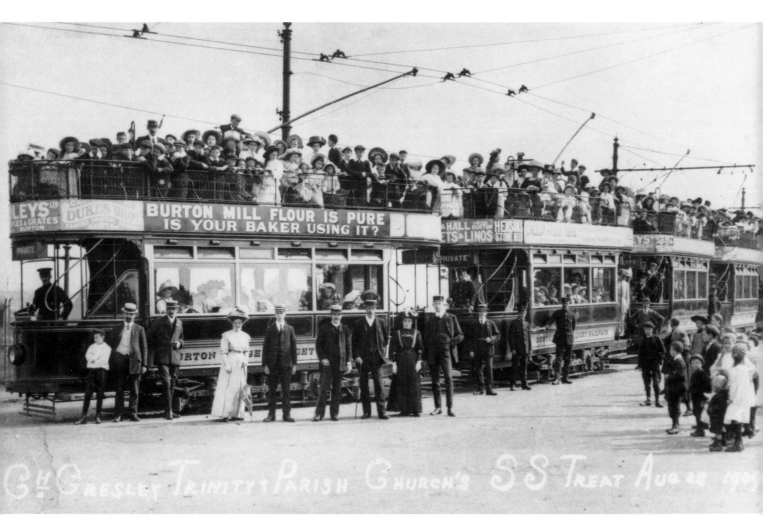

Relatively few tramways in Britain were owned by main-line railway companies; one of these was the ten-mile long 3ft 6in gauge Burton & Ashby Light Railway that provided a link between the tramway operated by Burton Corporation and Ashby-de-la-Zouch. With a Light Railway Order having been obtained in 1902, the first section of line – to Swadlincote – opened on 13 June 1906 with the remainder – to Ashby – following on 2 July the same year. In order to operate the tramway, Brush supplied a total of twenty open-top cars on the same manufacturer's AA four-wheel trucks. Nos 1-13 were delivered in 1905 whilst Nos 14-20 came the following year. This view – taken in August 1909 – records a quarter of the fleet, with No 15 leading, being utilised by the congregation of Trinity Church, Gresley, for a Sunday School outing. The Burton & Ashby ceased operation on 19 February 1927. Following abandonment, the lower deck of sister car No 14 was sold for use in a garden at Gresley; rescued for preservation in 1968 and restored using a Brill 21E truck from Lisbon, No 14 was exported to Detroit in 1980 where it was used as a heritage tram until 2003. Stored thereafter, the car was rescued in 2014 and repatriated to the UK. Moved to Statfold Barn, the tram has been regauged to 3ft 0in so that it can operate under battery power on some of the museum's track. *D.W.K. Jones Collection/Online Transport Archive*

In 1907, UEC supplied Sheffield Corporation with fifteen new trams – Nos 258-272 – the first trams delivered new to the operator fitted with open-balcony top covers. Originally fitted with M&G Radial four-wheel trucks, these were replaced by Peckham P22 trucks between 1918 and 1920, following the successful test replacement on No 259 in 1911. Between 1924 and 1927, all were rebuilt as fully-enclosed before being renumbered 336-50 in 1937. Four of the type – Nos 337/38/40/41 – were withdrawn before the Second World War but the remainder survived the war, being withdrawn between 1947 and the mid-1950s; three – Nos 346/49/50 – were to have subsequent careers as works cars with Nos 349 and 350 surviving until 1960 in these new roles. No 264 – pictured here after rebuilding in 1926 but before renumbering as No 342 in 1937 – is captured descending High Street passed the C&A store as it approaches Fitzalan Square. The store itself opened on 18 March 1932 but was destroyed during a bombing raid on 12 December 1940. Withdrawn and preserved in 1956, the car has been based at Beamish since 1973. Initially restored to a non-appropriate open-top condition in 1975, it was returned to an open-balcony condition in 1989. *J. Joyce Collection/Online Transport Archive*

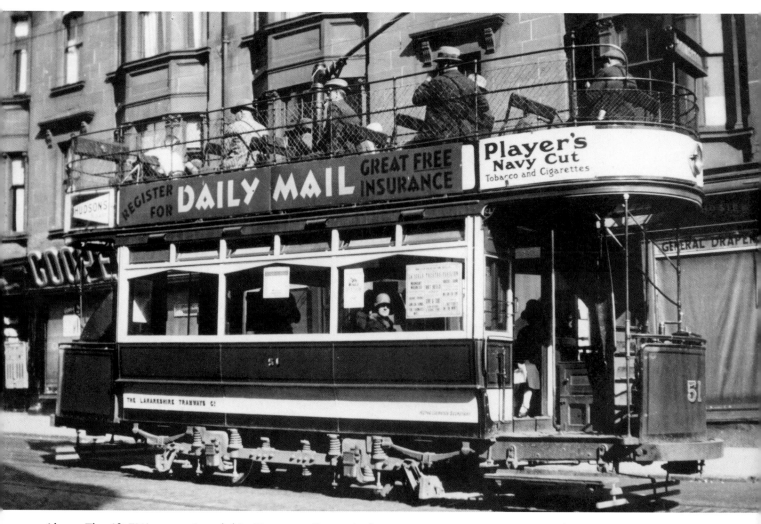

Above: The **4ft** 7¾in gauge Lanarkshire Tramways Co acquired seven open-top cars – Nos 47-53 – from UEC in 1908 on M&G 21EM four-wheel trucks. Nicknamed 'Dreadnoughts', the batch was largely used on workmen's duties and occasionally as works cars. Designed Type C, all were rebuilt in the company's workshops during 1921 and 1922 and redesignated as Type M. Typical of the type following rebuilding is No 51, pictured here at Blantyre in 1929. The last of the Lanarkshire trams operated on 14 February 1931 and the fleet was disposed of. No 53, which had been used as a source of spares, ended up on a farm at Beith, from where its remains were rescued in 1986. Transferred to the Summerlee Heritage Trust at Coatbridge and restored using the regauged truck from Oporto No 150, the car's restoration was completed in the spring of 1995. No 53 remains based at Summerlee. *Barry Cross Collection/Online Transport Archive*

Opposite: The **single** largest type of trams operated by any tramway in the British Isles was the LCC's 'E/1' class; with those built for the LCC built between 1907 and 1930 as well as those of a similar design constructed for use by other London operators – all of which passed to the LPTB in 1933 – well over 1,000 were constructed. The trams were supplied by a number of builders – including English Electric, Hurst Nelson and the LCC itself – with the bogies coming from a number of suppliers including M&G and Heenan &Froude. The story of the evolution and operation of the 'E/1' class is complex – suffice to note here that a number underwent the LPTB's 'Rehabilitation' programme of the late 1930s, whilst others received platform vestibules during the 1930s once Metropolitan Police restrictions on their use were lifted. Whilst a number were withdrawn as a result of the contraction of the tramway system during the late 1930s and others were lost as a result of enemy action during the Second World War, many of the type survived through until the final programme of tramcar abandonment – 'Operation Tramaway' – between 1950 and 1952. Only one of the type survived into preservation initially; this was No 1025 – seen here whilst operating on route 74 passing Catford bus depot on 10 November 1951 – which was retained by London Transport following withdrawal in January 1952. No 1025 was one of a batch built by the LCC itself on Hurst Nelson bogies during 1907 and 1908; fitted with a fully-enclosed upper-deck from new, the car was equipped with platform vestibules in January 1938. Now part of the London Transport Museum collection, the car has been based at the museum's Acton store since February 2006. *John Meredith/Online Transport Archive*

In 1909 and 1910, the City of Hull Tramways constructed fourteen open-balcony cars – Nos 123-36 – on M&G 21EM four-wheel trucks at its Liverpool Street Works. As with the Milnes-built cars, all were rebuilt as fully enclosed between 1920 and 1931. Hull tramways adopted – as did Doncaster Corporation – unusual centre-grooved track; the way that this track was laid meant that passengers benefited from a smoother ride. Much of the Hull system had been converted to trolleybus operation before the Second World War and two of the surviving three routes were also to succumb during the war; this resulted in the withdrawal of a number of trams. Rather than be scrapped, forty-two redundant Hull cars were sold to Leeds Corporation in 1942 and in June 1945, after the final closure of the Hull system. One of the cars transferred was No 132 – seen here at the Beverley Road terminus pre-war in rebuilt form – which was one of those to migrate to the West Riding in 1942, where it became Leeds No 446. New originally in 1910, No 132 was rebuilt as fully enclosed in 1931 and was subsequently fitted with a second-hand truck. No 446 was used on an enthusiasts' tour on 21 October 1951, after which it was withdrawn (the last of the type to remain in service in Leeds). Preserved on a Peckham Cantilever truck salvaged from No 110A, No 446 was stored in Lancashire until May 1960 when it was transferred to Crich. After a brief period in storage at Clay Cross, the tram was moved on loan to Hull in March 1983, where it was externally restored as Hull No 132 and placed on display in the city's Streetlife Museum on a Brill 21E truck. *H.B. Priestley/NTM*

Between 1904 and 1930, Maidstone Corporation operated a small 3ft 6in gauge tramway that extended over almost 5½ route miles at its maximum. The fleet comprised seventeen open-top four-wheel cars, supplied between 1904 and 1906, and a solitary single-deck demi-car, No 18, supplied by UEC on an M&G 21E four-wheel truck in 1909. This car, which is pictured here alongside one of the open-top cars outside the depot, was designed for one-man operation on the Tovil route, which had opened on 16 October 1907; traffic levels on this route had not met expectations and so No 18 was acquired. It remained on the route until 1919, when traffic had grown sufficiently to necessitate the use of a double-deck car, and No 18 was effectively withdrawn. It saw little service thereafter and was not used again after 1926. Sold two years later, its body was rediscovered in Winchelsea in 1970 in use as a caravan and it was subsequently secured for preservation. Now stored as a grounded body in Dover, the tram remains unrestored. *Barry Cross Collection/ Online Transport Archive*

As a result of opposition to the erection of overhead within the town, when Wolverhampton Corporation undertook the electrification of the tramways that it acquired on 1 May 1900, it adopted the Lorain surface contact system. Amongst the trams that the corporation acquired for operation using this were six – Nos 44-49 – open-top cars supplied by UEC during 1908 and 1909 on M&G 21EM four-wheel trucks. The first of the batch is pictured here in original condition. All six were equipped with open-balcony top covers and enclosed lower-deck vestibules. The final trams to operate using the Lorain system ran in 1921 and, thereafter, the surviving trams operated using conventional overhead until the final conversion of the system on 30 November 1928. The body of No 49 was sold after closure. Spending some time as a coffin store, its remains were secured in 1976 and restored to operational condition at the Black Country Museum with work being completed in 2012. Although restored to its original open-top condition, the car is, however, fitted with a trolleypole. *Barry Cross Collection/Online Transport Archive*

In 1910, UEC supplied West Ham Corporation with a batch of six cars – Nos 101-06 – fitted with Peckham R7 Radial four-wheel trucks. This manufacturer's view records No 102 when new and shows the unusual body with which the tram was originally fitted, the six arched windows on the lower deck and the three drop windows on the upper. Fitted originally with transverse seats on the lower deck, these were replaced by longitudinal seating before the First World War and the cars were further rebuilt in the early 1920s, with three-window lower decks and with their trucks made rigid. Initially fitted with plough carriers, these were removed in the late 1920s and one final change saw the cars rehabilitated with upholstered seats during 1929 and 1930. All six remained in service following the creation of the LPTB, becoming Nos 289-94, but the programme to convert the routes in East London to trolleybus operation saw Nos 289/92-94 withdrawn in 1937, leaving Nos 290 and 291 to follow in March 1938 following the conversion of route 99A. Whilst No 291 was scrapped, No 290 was transferred to New Cross depot for preservation. It is now part of the London Transport Museum Collection and on display at Covent Garden. *UEC/Barry Cross Collection/Online Transport Archive*

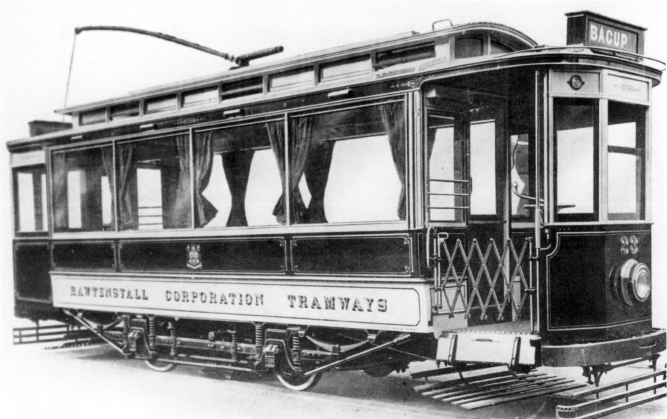

Above: **Extending at** its maximum extent to almost 5¾ route miles, the small system operated by the City of Carlisle Tramways Co Ltd opened originally on 13 June 1900. The initial fleet of 3ft 6in gauge trams comprised three single-deck and twelve open-top double-deck cars all supplied by ERTCW all on Brill 21E four-wheel trucks. In 1912, the entire fleet was replaced by eight double-deck cars – Nos 1-8 – and four single-deck cars – Nos 9-12 – all built by UEC, again all using Brill 21E trucks. One of the former – No 7 – is pictured here heading west towards Newtown along Newtown Road. Following the conversion of the Carlisle system on 21 November 1921, the trams were disposed of. None were preserved at the time but recently the lower-deck body of one – number unknown – was retrieved in a poor condition with a view to restoration. Now owned by the Workington Transport Heritage Trust, the tram awaits restoration. *Barry Cross Collection/Online Transport Archive*

Opposite above: **In the** knowledge that the corporation was to take over the operation of the Selly Oak and Kings Heath routes from the City of Birmingham Tramways Co Ltd in July 1911, and that the company's cars were in a poor condition, Birmingham Corporation decided to add a further forty trams to an existing order for sixty open-balcony cars placed with UEC. Nos 361-400, fitted with the same manufacturer's flexible-axle four-wheel trucks, were all delivered between November 1911 and February 1912. Between 1917 and 1923, five of the batch – Nos 361/67/68/75/79 – operated as single-deck cars with their original top covers removed. Of the forty cars, all were in service at the start of the Second World War but numbers were reduced by enemy action and withdrawals during the war – Nos 362/84/90-92/98/99 all succumbing (the body of No 392 being transferred to the truck of No 393) – with the surviving cars all being withdrawn following the conversion of the Washwood Heath, Alum Rock and Lozells services on 30 September 1950. No 395 – seen here on a service towards Small Heath on route 78 on 7 July 1950 – was preserved following a request from the corporation's City Museum & Art Gallery Department. It was on display at the Birmingham Museum of Science & Industry on Newhall Street for many years and is now an exhibit in the city's Thinktank science museum, part of the Millennium Point complex. *Photograph by G.F. Douglas, courtesy of A. D. Packer*

Opposite below: **Between 15** May 1909 and 31 March 1932, Rawtenstall Corporation operated a 4ft 0in gauge network that extended over 11¾ route miles at its peak. In 1912, the existing fleet of sixteen open-top four-wheel cars was supplemented by two open-balcony cars, Nos 17 and 18, and a batch of six single-deck cars supplied, like the earlier eighteen, by UEC. Nos 19-24 were fitted with Preston flexible four-wheel trucks. No 23 is pictured here in a manufacturer's photograph taken when new. Like all of the Rawtenstall fleet, No 23 was withdrawn in 1932 following the conversion of the system to bus operation. However, some four decades later, its body was rescued with a view to restoration. Based for a period in London, where the body was dismantled into a kit of parts, the tram's remains – now housed on a standard gauge track from Oporto – have been stored at the Heaton Park Tramway since 2010 with a view to long term restoration. *Barry Cross Collection/Online Transport Archive*

Above and opposite: **The LCC** 'E/1' class has already been encountered – see the narrative on No 1025 on page 76 – but a second car of the type also survives: No 1622 at the NTM. The final batch acquired before the First World War were 200 – Nos 1477-676 – built by Brush on bogies supplied by Heenan & Froude and new during 1911 and 1912. All underwent the Pullmanisation programme of the late 1920s, with some thirty-five being further modified during the 'Rehabilitation' programme of the mid to late 1930s. The majority – but not No 1622 – were also fitted with lower deck vestibule windscreens. Towards the end of its career, No 1622 would have looked similar to No 1539, pictured here on route 6 – a service that linked Southwark with Tooting Junction via Elephant & Castle and Clapham – prior to the Second World War. All of the non-windscreen 'E/1s' were withdrawn by 1940, although a number – including Nos 1539 and 1622 – were stored during the war in case they were needed to replaced trams damaged or destroyed by enemy action. In the event, No 1622 was not returned to service and its body was disposed of in August 1946, being one of a number of redundant 'E/1s' transferred to Hayling Island in August 1946. The lower deck of No 1622 escaped the fate of the other bodies on Hayling Island, as many were soon dismantled, when it was relocated to Liss in Hampshire, where it was rediscovered in 1969. Rescued a decade later, the tram underwent a long restoration project, completed in 1997, that saw it appear in 'Rehab' form – as illustrated in the view of No 1771 at Lavender Hill, Latchmere Road, on 25 June 1949 – combining the restored lower deck of No 1622, some parts from a second body included in the upper deck and the bogies recovered from 'Feltham' No 2138 (later Leeds No 554 [517]) following its scrapping on the Middleton Railway. Work on its restoration commenced under the auspices of the LCCTT with work being finished at Crich. No 1622 remains part of the NTM's operational fleet. *W.J. Wyse/LRTA (London Area) Collection/John Meredith (both Online Transport Archive)*

Although authorised during the First World War to operate double-deck trams, it was not until the mid-1930s that the Llandudno &
Colwyn Bay Electric Railway actually exercised these powers. In 1936, the company acquired ten open-top bogie cars from
Bournemouth Corporation. Of these, one – Bournemouth No 85 – had been built by UEC in 1914 whilst the remainder had all been
supplied by Brush between 1921 and 1926; all were fitted with Brill 22E bogies. No 85 was modified in 1920 by the addition of platform
vestibules. By the early 1950s, the finances of the tramway were deteriorating and the line closed on 24 March 1956 – the last 3ft 6in
tramway in Britain to be abandoned – and, although there were attempts to raise funds to preserve it, these came to nothing. No 6 –
which is seen here turning at Palladium Corner in Llandudno from Gloddaeth Street into Mostyn Street – was secured for preservation,
for £75, by a local man who presented it to the Museum of British Transport at Clapham. Displayed there until the museum closed in
1973, ownership passed to the Science Museum, which placed the car on loan to Bournemouth Corporation. Restored to its original
Bournemouth livery, the car was displayed in the Bournemouth area for almost forty years until 2012 when, following the closure of its
home museum, ownership was transferred to the NTM. The tram was transferred to Crich on 25 August 2017. Unsuitable for operation
at Crich due to its gauge, the car is now on display as a typical narrow-gauge car. *John McCann/Online Transport Archive*

In 1914 the Blackpool & Fleetwood Tramroad Co acquired four new single-deck cars – Nos 38-41 – from UEC; fitted with the same manufacturer's McGuire-type equal-wheel bogies, the four cars were the last new trams acquired by the company. Passing to Blackpool Corporation on 1 January 1920, the quartet became Nos 112-15. No 114 was to receive upholstered seating in 1926 and replacement motors in 1928; the late 1920s also saw its original controllers replaced. Withdrawn in 1936, No 40 was converted into a works car – No 5 – and it is in this condition that the car is recorded at Talbot Square in August 1951. It was restored back to Blackpool & Fleetwood No 40 for the 75th anniversary of Blackpool's tramways in 1960, having been in store since 1954, and transferred to Crich in October 1963. Over the past fifty years, No 40 has seen operation at Heaton Park and Beamish as well as its home town; since the autumn of 2019 it has again been based at the National Tramway Museum. *Phil Tatt/Online Transport Archive*

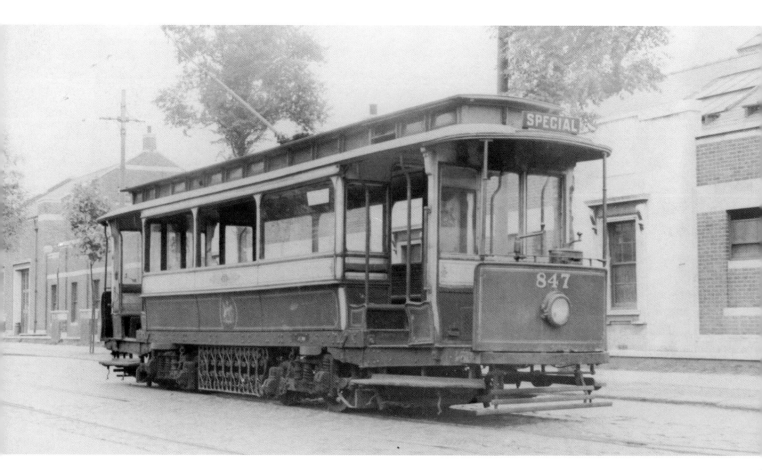

***Above*: The use** of trailer cars on British tramways was not common but one of the most significant users was the LCC. Although there were earlier experiments, the first regular use came in 1913 when eight converted horse cars were introduced to the Eltham route; however, it was during the First World War when trailer operation expanded considerably with 150 new trailers – Nos T9-T158 – being supplied by Brush from 1915 onwards in order to increase capacity to meet wartime demand. In 1922, the decision was made to cease trailer operation and the last services were operated on 17 April 1924. The bodies of the withdrawn trailers were disposed of, many finding new uses as holiday chalets. Typical of the Brush-built trailers is No T26, seen here at the Oval, Kennington; sister car No T24 was converted into a horse drawn caravan and ended its days on a farm near Abbeyleix, in County Laois, Ireland. Its body was preserved in September 1982 by the Transport Museum Society of Ireland and used as the basis of a reconstructed Dublin open-top car No 224 (mounted on a road trailer). In this condition, the restored tram is now on display at Howth. *Barry Cross Collection/Online Transport Archive*

***Opposite above*: In order** to operate the future route 53 – the 8¼-mile service between Cheetham Hill Road and Stretford Road – with its low railway bridges at Stanley Grove and Pottery Lane (which made it unsuitable for double-deck cars), Manchester Corporation acquired a number of single-deck combination cars all of which were equipped with Brill 22E bogies: Nos 512-36 came from G.F. Milnes & Co in 1903; Nos 649-68 from UEC in 1907; Nos 763-67 were constructed in the corporation's own Hyde Road Works in 1914; and, Nos 836-47 came from English Electric during 1920 and 1921. In addition, ten similar cars were taken over from the Middleton Electric Traction Co in 1925; these had originally been built by Brush in 1902. Typical of the single-deck cars is No 847, illustrated here. The conversion of route 53 to bus operation during March and April 1930 rendered the combination cars redundant and all were taken out of service between then and the outbreak of the Second World War; only one survived the war – No 847 – which was scrapped in 1947 (despite hopes that it might have been preserved). Following withdrawal in 1930, the body of sister car No 765 was sold to a farm at Linthwaite near Huddersfield, from where it was rescued and transferred to Crich in June 1960. Restoration commenced following a move to Stretford in July 1963 and was completed, using bogies from an ex-Hill of Howth car, in April 1977. Now based on the Heaton Park Tramway, No 765 has also spent time at both Blackpool and Beamish. *D.W.K. Jones Collection/Online Transport Archive*

***Opposite below*: In 1915,** the Great Central Railway acquired four additional single-deck trams – Nos 13-16 – at its Dukinfield Works, using parts and equipment supplied by Brush, to supplement its fleet on the Grimsby & Immingham line. Fitted with Brush equal-wheel bogies, these were similar to the earlier cars – Nos 1-4 of 1911 and 9-12 of 1913 – that provided the majority of services over the tramway through GCR and London & North Eastern Railway ownership until the line was taken over by British Railways in 1948. At 54ft 2in in length, these trams were amongst the longest first-generation trams to operate in the country. Of the GCR cars, eight survived through until the final closure of the line on 1 July 1961. No 14, which had undergone a minor rebuild following an accident in January 1958, was preserved by the TMS and transferred to the society's store at Clay Cross in November 1961. Stored for more than quarter of a century, it was loaned to the National Railway Museum in August 1988 and cosmetically restored before returning to Crich in June 1990. The car, which has never operated at Crich and remains on static display in the museum, is seen here in June 1956. *Phil Tatt/Online Transport Archive*

The last new tramcars acquired by the Paisley District Tramways Co were five open-top double-deck cars – Nos 68-72 – supplied by Hurst Nelson in 1919 on solid forged four-wheel trucks. In August 1923, these became Glasgow Corporation Nos 1068-72. Like a number of the other ex-Paisley cars, No 1068 underwent modification by its new owners. Its truck was replaced by a Brill 21E and in June 1924 it was fitted with an open-balcony top cover. A further rebuild, in May 1931, saw it converted to fully-enclosed, looking similar in style to the Glasgow 'Standard' type. By the late 1940s, the surviving ex-Paisley cars, Nos 1053-72, were scheduled for early withdrawal with only three – Nos 1062/68/69 – still operational, from Elderslie depot, by 1953. Following withdrawal, No 1068 was retained and used as a shunter at Elderslie, pending possible preservation, until that depot closed on 11 May 1957. The tram was then stored at Dalmarnock prior to presentation to the Scottish Tramway Museum Society. No 1068 was transferred to Crich in September 1960 and was subsequently restored to its open-top and open lower-deck platform guise as Paisley No 68. Here, No 1068 is seen at the terminus at Millerston on 23 March 1949. *Michael H. Waller*

In 1920, Wallasey Corporation took delivery of a batch of ten cars – Nos 69-78 – that were to prove the last new trams acquired by the corporation. These were built by Brush and fitted with Peckham P22 four-wheel trucks. Like all of the trams acquired by Wallasey since 1905, the ten cars were fitted with short 'Bellamy'-type top covers from new; the original open-top cars were also fitted with similar covers shortly after entering service. No 78 – seen here outside the corporation's Seaview Road depot – was the last tram in Britain to be constructed with such a top cover. Withdrawn following the final conversion of the Wallasey system on 30 November 1933, the body of No 78 was sold to a farm in North Wales from where it was rescued for preservation by the Merseyside Tramway Preservation Society for restoration at the Wirral Transport Museum. The restoration work was completed during the summer of 2002 and the tram remains operational on the Birkenhead tramway. *Barry Cross Collection/Online Transport Archive*

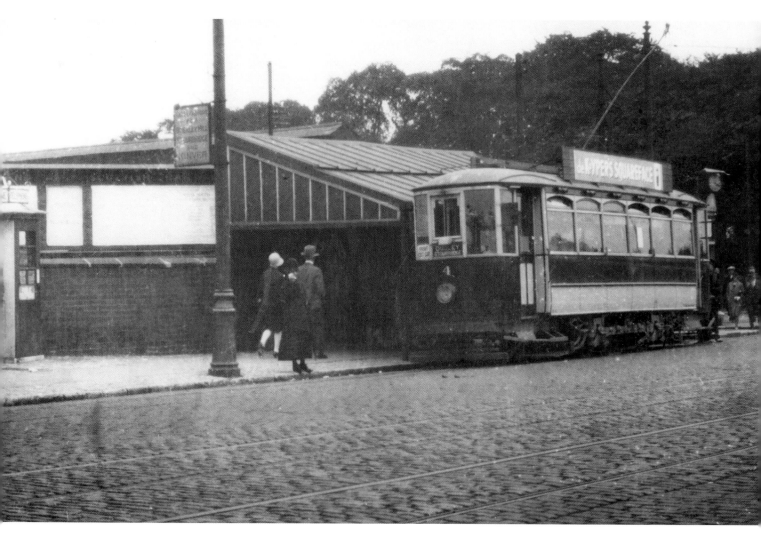

Above: **The Black** Country had a complex 3ft 6in gauge network of lines – both corporation and company operated – with the latter comprising four subsidiaries of BET, operating latterly under the banner of the Birmingham & Midland Tramways Joint Committee. One of this quartet was the Dudley, Stourbridge & District Electric Traction Co Ltd and, during 1919 and 1920, this company acquired fifteen new single-deck trams built at the committee's Tividale workshops on Brush flexible four-wheel trucks. Typical of this batch is No 4, pictured here on the siding situated at the terminus at Dudley station; the double track in the foreground led along Birmingham Road towards Birmingham and West Bromwich. The last trams operated on the Dudley, Stourbridge & District on 1 March 1930 and the fleet was subsequently disposed of. Sister car No 5 – new in 1920 – was converted into a summerhouse at Bennett's Hill and was rescued for preservation in 1973. Fully restored at the Black Country Museum, it entered service there, using a Brill 21E four-wheel, truck in 1980. Having been fully overhauled by the Llangollen Railway between 2012 and 2017, the tram is operational again. *Barry Cross Collection/ Online Transport Archive*

Opposite: **After the** First World War, English Electric supplied Nottingham Corporation with two batches of trams. The first twenty-five – Nos 156-80 – were open-balcony cars on Preston Flexible four-wheel trucks as illustrated by No 179, pictured in Market Place in August 1936 shortly before the system's final conversion (on 5 September). The lower deck of one of the batch – No 166 – was sold following withdrawal in 1934 to be converted into accommodation at a farm at Hagworthingham in Lincolnshire. The surviving lower deck, with its surviving enclosed vestibules, was rescued in March 2007, after planning consent was granted for its replacement, and transferred to the NTM's Clay Cross store. It remains there, in an unrestored condition as a possible future restoration project. The NTM also has parts of two other Nottingham trams: the lower-deck body of No 45, built by ERTCW in 1901, survives as a grounded body whilst one end vestibule of No 121, a UEC-built car of 1908, is also stored at Clay Cross. *Barry Cross Collection/Online Transport Archive*

Above: **The last** open-balcony cars acquired by Leeds Corporation were delivered in the decade from 1913 until 1923; Nos 293-369 were all constructed at Kirkstall Road Works and fitted with four-wheel trucks from Brush, Hurst Nelson and Peckham. All of the cars constructed post-war – Nos 340-69 – were converted to fully-enclosed between 1935 and 1940 as were two of the older cars – Nos 322 and 339 – in 1938 and 1942 respectively. The remainder remained in open-balcony form until withdrawal. Known as 'Converts', the first of the fully-enclosed cars was withdrawn in 1945 and all had been withdrawn by the end of 1951. No 343 – pictured here at Kirkstall Abbey – was typical of the 'Convert' cars; it was withdrawn in April 1949. Sister car No 345 – new in March 1921 when fitted with a Hurst Nelson 21E truck and fully enclosed in January 1939 – was withdrawn in September 1948, having originally entered the works two months earlier for overhaul. It was converted into a works car for use initially at Kirkstall Road and subsequently at Swinegate and, as such, avoided the fate of the rest of the type. Acquired by the Leeds Transport Historical Society in 1959, the car was transferred to Crich in December 1959 with a view to restoration into its original open-balcony condition. Stored at Clay Cross from 1982, the car was lucky to survive when the store was set on fire by vandals in 1999. Returned to Crich in 2002, the car was fully restored to its 'Convert' condition and in the Prussian blue and white livery in which it operated from 1927. The restored tram entered service in 2006 and remains part of the NTM's operational fleet. *W.A. Camwell/National Tramway Museum*

Opposite above: **Between 22 September** 1904 and 11 July 1929, Swindon Corporation operated a small – 3¾ route mile – 3ft 6in gauge system. Twelve open-top trams were supplied between 1904 and 1906 but it was not until 1921 when the system received its thirteenth - and last – new car. This was No 13, seen here at the Centre turning from Regent Street into Fleet Street, which was built by English Electric; fitted with a Preston Standard four-wheel truck, No 13 was the only Swindon tram to be fitted with enclosed lower-deck vestibules from new. Following withdrawal in 1929, the body of No 13 was sold to a Chiseldon-based undertaker and was used for the storage of coffins, timber and paint. Passing into new ownership in 1957, after the undertaker's death, the body was salvaged in 1982 and has subsequently been through various hands in an unrestored condition before arriving at Coleford, in the Forest of Dean, where it has been stored in the open for some twenty years. At the time of writing, its future is uncertain. *Barry Cross Collection/Online Transport Archive*

Opposite below: **The last** new trams acquired by the 3ft 6in gauge Cheltenham & District Light Railway Co, a company that operated almost 10½ routes miles in and around the town, were three open-top double-deck cars supplied by English Electric in 1921 on Preston-built Peckham Pendulum trucks. The original order had been for four trams, but the final car was diverted to the Leamington & Warwick Electrical Co Ltd, a fellow subsidiary of Balfour Beatty. The three cars were destined for a relatively short operational life as the final trams ran in Cheltenham on 31 December 1930. One of the trio, No 23, is seen here outside the company's St Mark's depot. The body of sister car No 21, which had been used as a garden storehouse at Hunscot Farm since withdrawal, was rescued for preservation by the Tramcar No 21 Group in September 1961 and transferred to Crich, following restoration and fitting of a standard gauge, in 1965. Never operated at Crich, ownership was transferred (subject a reversion clause) to Bournemouth Borough Council in 1981 and then was transferred without its standard gauge truck, to Mallard Road. However, there was little progress on the proposed museum at Bournemouth and, in 1992, a further transfer saw ownership transferred to Cheltenham Borough Council. The body of the tram is currently in store in its 'as restored' condition awaiting a full restoration. *Barry Cross Collection/Online Transport Archive*

Above: **By June** 1922, when Glasgow 'Standard' No 22 was delivered, the design of the type had evolved to include enclosed lower-deck enclosed platforms and open-balcony top covers and it was in this condition that No 22 emerged from Coplawhill Works. Rebuilt as fully enclosed in April 1930, No 22 – seen here on 31 October 1958 at the junction of Argyle Street and Union Street whilst heading towards Farme Cross with a service on route 17 – was withdrawn towards the end of 1960 and owed its survival initially through use as a depot shunter at Maryhill. Following withdrawal, it was restored at Coplawhill to its original – Phase III – condition with an open-balcony top cover. Preserved in 1962, the tram was transferred to Crich, where it was to be one of the first electric trams to operate following the first use of the overhead on 6 June 1964. A stalwart of the NTM fleet, No 22 made a brief return to its home city in 1988 when it was one of the trams used at that year's Garden Festival in Glasgow. *Hamish Stevenson/Online Transport Archive*

Opposite above: **In 1923,** Blackpool Corporation constructed a combined railgrinder and snowplough at Rigby Road. Originally No 1, the car was fitted with a 21E-type four-wheel truck supplied by the Manchester-based Malleable Steel Castings Co (1909) Ltd. Renumbered 2 in 1968, it was further renumbered to 752 in 1972 and it is in this guise that the tram is pictured in Rigby Road depot in October 1975. Surviving in service until the early years of this century, No 752 was transferred to the Heaton Park Tramway in 2008; based on the East Lancashire Railway for two years from 2011, the car is now again based – on static display – at Heaton Park. *Philip Hanson/Online Transport Archive*

Opposite below: **Swansea, like** Cardiff, suffered from a number of low railway bridges which required the use of single-deck or open-top double-deck cars until the development of lowbridge fully-enclosed double-deck cars in the early 1920s. Following Cardiff's successful development of such a car, the standard-gauge Swansea Improvements & Tramways Co Ltd, which operated a network extending over 5½ route miles at its peak, acquired eleven fully-enclosed lowbridge cars – No 5-15 – from Brush in 1923. In this view, the first of the batch can be seen on High Street. These were fitted with Peckham P22 four-wheel trucks and were followed by two further similar cars – Nos 3 and 4 – two years later. Following the final conversion of the Swansea system on 29 June 1937, the fleet was disposed of. The body of sister car No 14 ended up at a farm near Ammanford from where it was rescued in 1977; the tram was restored using the upper deck of a second car – No 12 – allied to a truck – a Brill 79EX2 – and electrical equipment from Belgium. The restored car is now on display at the National Waterfront Museum in Swansea. *Barry Cross Collection/Online Transport Archive*

High Street, Swansea

Until it was bypassed in the 1930s, the Bargate in Southampton represented a significant problem for the corporation's trams. Its low height meant that conventional covered top trams were unsuitable and this meant that, until the early 1920s, the fleet relied on open-top cars – such as No 45 seen on page 53 – to operate the majority of services. However, from the early 1920s, the corporation developed trams with low floors and smaller diameter wheels that permitted, with a dome roof, fully-enclosed trams to pass through the gate. The last open-top cars built for the corporation were five, including No 3 (in 1924), which were delivered between 1920 and 1924 on Brill 21E four-wheel trucks. All five were rebuilt with Bargate-style domed roofs in 1925, being renumbered 7-11. Three of the batch, including No 11 (ex No 3) illustrated here post-war, received replacement Peckham P35 trucks. The last Southampton trams were withdrawn on 31 December 1949 and a significant number were sold to Leeds Corporation for further use (although the majority never re-entered service). One of those not sold to Leeds was No 11, which eventually found its way to Alresford, in Hampshire, where it was used as a children's playhouse. Rescued in October 1979, the tram is currently under restoration in Southampton; when completed it will be the only Bargate roofed tram to survive. *Barry Cross Collection/Online Transport Archive*

The early history of the Blackpool 'Standard' cars is complex; seven of the type – Nos 146-52 – were constructed as new trams by Hurst Nelson of Motherwell but, for accounting purposes (they were allocated to the Revenue rather than the Capital account), the remaining thirty-five were all notionally rebuilds of older cars and constructed by the corporation itself at Rigby Road. All bar the last two of the type – Nos 51 and 177 – were completed with open lower-deck vestibules and all were initially built with open-balcony top covers. Completed in 1924, No 143 – seen here – is now the oldest surviving of the corporation-built cars. It was modified in December 1929 by the addition of lower-deck vestibules and was rebuilt as fully enclosed in February 1932. Surviving in passenger service until October 1957, the car was then converted into works use – as No 3 – in July 1958. It reverted to open-balcony form in October 1961 and was renumbered 753 in March 1972. Finally withdrawn in June 1990, the tram was preserved. It returned to Rigby Road in October 2013 where work is now in hand restoring the car to its original – i.e. open lower-deck vestibule – form. *W.S. Eades Collection/Online Transport Archive*

Above: Following on from the construction of four experimental fully-enclosed cars – Nos 366-69 – in its own workshops between 1918 and 1921, Sheffield Corporation acquired no fewer than 150 fully enclosed cars between 1919 and 1927. All were equipped with Peckham P22 four-wheel trucks with Brush supplying the bodies for Nos 36-60 and 376-450 and the Cravens Carriage & Wagon Co Ltd those for Nos 451-500. Two cars – Nos 430 and 483 – were destroyed by enemy action during the Second World War (and replaced by new cars) whilst No 493 was withdrawn in 1946. The remainder were all withdrawn between 1950 and 1957. Although none was preserved on withdrawal, the lower decks of three of the type survive in various guises. Part of the lower decks of Nos 419 – built in 1924 – and 442 – also of 1924 – are grounded at the Trolleybus Museum at Sandtoft whilst part of the lower deck of No 460 (of 1926) – seen here heading down High Street towards Fitzalan Square with a service to Intake – is now based at the South Yorkshire Transport Museum, Aldwarke, having been withdrawn originally in February 1950 and rescued from a location near Scunthorpe in May 1987. *Barry Cross Collection/Online Transport Archive*

Opposite above: **Seven of** Blackpool 'Standard' cars were completed at Hurst Nelson in 1924; like all the type, these were fitted with McGuire-type bogies. Of these seven, only one – No 147 – now survives and this car is pictured here at Station Road, South Shore, in late October 1950. The car was fitted with lower-deck vestibules in June 1933 and was rebuilt as fully enclosed in May 1940 as one of the last five to be so modified. Withdrawn in October 1966 as one of the last 'Standards' in service alongside Nos 158-60, No 147 was preserved and exported to the USA in September 1967. The 'Standard' was destined to remain in the USA until late 2000 when, following an exchange for 'Boat' No 606, it was returned to the UK. It now forms part of the Blackpool heritage fleet, having spent a year during 2016 and 2017 at Beamish. *Peter N. Williams/Online Transport Archive*

Opposite below: **In June** 1924, after more than twenty years, the final Glasgow 'Standard' car – No 1088 – emerged from Coplawhill Works. A total of 312 Phase III 'Standard' cars – wider lower saloon with hexagonal dashes on longer 7ft 0in 21E wheelbase four-wheel trucks supplied by either Brill or Brush – were delivered between 1910 and 1924. As delivered, these cars were fitted with lower-deck enclosed vestibules but open-balcony top covers; progressively they were rebuilt as fully enclosed. In No 1088's case, this work was completed in January 1933. The car, seen here outside Newlands Depot on 16 April 1954, was preserved by the corporation following withdrawal in June 1961, having been temporarily restored to service following the disastrous Dalmarnock depot fire three months earlier. It was last operated as part of the closure procession on 4 September 1962. Today, the car in on display in the city's Riverside Museum. *R.B. Parr/NTM*

Above: **Between April** 1923 and August 1930, Norwich Electric Tramways, a subsidiary of the New General Traction Co, rebodied thirty-four of the existing open-top four-wheel cars in the fleet using bodies supplied by English Electric. Two of the rebodied cars – Nos 38 and 41 – are pictured here alongside one of the cars – No 28 – that retained its original body through to withdrawal. The final 3ft 6in-gauge trams operated in the city on 10 December 1935 and, following conversion, bodies were sold off for £5 each. The lower deck of No 39, rebuilt in 1924, was discovered in the mid-1960s at Heacham, near Hunstanton, and was rescued by members of the EATMS and transferred to Carlton Colville. Used initially as a temporary tearoom and then as a shelter for the museum's East Suffolk Light Railway, there were plans – never fulfilled – to convert the car into a carriage for the railway. In the event, the body was sold and has been restored to form part of a cottage at Acle. Curiously, the body of the original No 39 – new from Brush in 1900 – was also identified in the 1970s in use as a garden shed. It is also still believed to be extant. *Hugh Nicol/NTM*

Opposite above: **The last** new trams acquired by Lytham St Annes Corporation were ten open-balcony 'Pullman' cars – Nos 31-40 – that were supplied by English Electric on Peckham P22 four-wheel trucks in 1924. The tramway, which extended over some 6¼ route miles, had been operated by the Blackpool, St Annes & Lytham Tramways Co Ltd until taken by St Annes UDC on 28 October 1920; it became Lytham St Annes Corporation two years later. The last trams that the corporation acquired were all second-hand. The final Lytham trams operated on 28 April 1937 and the fleet – including No 43 seen here – was disposed of. The lower deck was subsequently rescued for preservation. Initially, there was a possibility that the body might be used to create a railway carriage for use on the West Lancashire Light Railway but it was acquired by Robert Mortimer for eventual restoration as a tram. Work on the lower deck was undertaken prior to it being relocated to Rigby Road on 24 January 2016 on long-term loan to the Blackpool Heritage Trust. The restoration of No 43 is considered to be a long-term project. *R. Elliott/TLRS*

Opposite below: **Constructed at** Rigby Road in 1925, Blackpool No 144 was to remain an open-balcony car throughout its operational career. Pictured here at Pleasure Beach in August 1952, the car was approaching the end of its career. Withdrawn in September the same year, No 144 was the first 'Standard' to be preserved – and the first Blackpool tram to cross the Atlantic – when it was sold to the Seashore Trolley Museum of Kennebunkport in Maine during March 1955. It is still based at Seashore and is, at the time of writing, undergoing restoration at the museum. *Phil Tatt/Online Transport Archive*

Above: **Between 1920** and 1928, Gateshead & District took delivery of twenty-five single-deck cars fitted with Brill 39E bogies; of these, Nos 1, 20 and 56-60 were supplied by Brush whilst the remainder were built in the company's own workshops at Sunderland Road. With the conversion of the Gateshead system (a process completed on 4 August 1951), nineteen of the cars were acquired by British Railways for its Grimsby & Immingham route. Of these, seventeen entered passenger service, one – No 4 – was severely damaged on delivery to BR and scrapped whilst the nineteenth was used as a works car. Gateshead No 10, which was new in 1925 and is seen here towards the end of its life on Tyneside, became Grimsby & Immingham No 26. Withdrawn with the closure of the tramway on 1 July 1961, No 26 was one of two ex-Gateshead cars – the other being No 20 (ex-Gateshead No 5 of 1927 – see page 111) – to be preserved. Stored initially at Clay Cross it was transferred to Consett in February 1968 for restoration for operation at Beamish, where it is still based, in Gateshead livery. *Barry Cross Collection/Online Transport Archive*

Opposite: **Between 1919** and 1931, Bradford Corporation constructed a total of eighty-one open-balcony four-wheel cars at Thornbury Works; these were predominantly fitted with 21E trucks. One of the batch – No 104 (which dated to 1925) – became the corporation's official last tram on 6 May 1950 and its pictured here suitably bedecked on that fateful day. Plans to preserve No 51 – another of the same batch which had been the last tram actually to operate in Bradford (it made a trip to Odsal on 8 May for official photographs) – came to nothing but the then manager of Bradford Northern RLFC offered to acquire No 104. Unfortunately, through a breakdown in communication, No 104 was stripped of much of its equipment, including the truck, and, following a brief sojourn in Baildon, only the body reached Odsal stadium in August 1950. There, for three years, it was used as a scoreboard. Rescued in April 1953, the tram was fully restored at Thornbury Works with a suitable 21E truck acquired from Sheffield Corporation; this had previously been used on snow plough No 358 in Sheffield. In July 1958, No 104 made its first run on the surviving track within Thornbury Works; it was used regularly until 1963. Problems with the electricity supply, however, curtailed its operation and it last operated in 1966. Stored in Thornbury Works thereafter, it was transferred to the city's Industrial Museum at Moorside Mills in the early 1970s; it remains on display there alongside one of the corporation's trolleybuses. *F.E.J. Ward/Online Transport Archive*

Blackpool 'Standard' No 40 was constructed at Rigby Road in 1926. As part of the programme to fit lower-deck vestibules, No 40 was so equipped in December 1931. Although the majority of the type survived into the post-war era – thirty-nine out of the forty-two cars constructed – withdrawals commenced again post-war and the open-balcony cars were all withdrawn by the end of the 1950s. No 40 had been taken out of service earlier but was reinstated in 1957 for use on an enthusiasts' tour and remained in service until it was withdrawn again. When finally taken out of the service on 12 January 1963, the car – seen here outside RIgby Road depot in 1960 – was the last open-balcony tram to operate on a British tramway. Transferred to Crich in October the same year, No 40 has been one of the mainstays of the NTM collection for almost sixty years, making one return visit to its home town – in 1985 – when it helped mark the centenary of the Blackpool system. *John McCann/Online Transport Archive*

Between 1923 and 1928, Leeds Corporation constructed forty trams – Nos 370-99 and 401-10 – at its Kirkstall Road Works; these were the first trams built for the corporation that were fully enclosed from new. All were fitted with four-wheel trucks supplied by a variety of manufacturers – Brill, Hurst Nelson, Peckham and EMB – with No 399 being built in 1925 and entering service in April 1926. When completed, No 399 – pictured here post-war awaiting departure from outside the Corn Exchange with a service on route 5 towards Beeston – was the last tram to emerge in the chocolate, white and yellow livery that had been a feature of the city's streets for more than three decades. It was to retain this scheme for only two years before being repainted in the new blue and white livery. Fitted with air brakes, the car was one of those used on the long route south-eastwards to Rothwell with its steep descent to the terminus. This route was one of the earlier conversions in Leeds – on 31 May 1932 – with No 39, and others of the type operating steeply-graded routes, including that to Beeston – which resulted in the type's later nickname of 'Beeston Air Brake' – prior to withdrawal in June 1951. It was then used for a period as the works shunter at Kirkstall Road before making one final journey – from Kirkstall Road to Swinegate for storage – in 1957 following the closure of Kirkstall Road to tram work. Acquired for preservation by members of the Leeds Transport Historical Society, the car was moved to Crich in August 1959 – the first passenger car to reach the new museum site. Stored away from the museum for a number of years, work commenced on its restoration in 1989 and, two years later, it returned to service restored to its original 1926 livery. *Barry Cross Collection/Online Transport Archive*

Above: **Constructed at** Rigby Road in October 1926, Blackpool 'Standard' No 49 was fitted with enclosed lower-deck vestibules in April 1932 and became fully-enclosed in March 1938. It is in this condition that the car is seen here at Talbot Square on 19 May 1950. Withdrawn in 1962, the car was acquired by the TMS and transferred to Crich in December that year. First run at the museum on 6 June 1964, No 49 was one of the earliest electric cars to operate at Crich. It last operated in service in 1992 and is currently on static display at the museum. *C. Carter/Online Transport Archive*

Opposite above: **In order** to supplement the existing illuminated cars, Blackpool modified two of the 1927 built 'Standards' – Nos 158 and 159 – in 1959 with exterior colour lights. The two cars – seen here outside Rigby Road depot in this condition – had originally been conventional cars, with open lower-deck vestibules and open-balcony top covers. Both were eventually to emerge as fully enclosed; No 159 was amongst the first of the type to be rebuilt as fully enclosed, with both the lower-deck vestibules and the upper-deck balconies being enclosed simultaneously in 1930. As modified, the two cars survived until October 1966 when all of the surviving 'Standards' were withdrawn. No 159 passed to the EATMS at Carlton Colville and has now been restored to its condition immediately prior to the fitting of the lighting in 1959; No 158 was acquired by the TMS primarily as a source of spare parts with the remains of the car being scrapped in 1978. *Harry Luff/Online Transport Archive*

Opposite below: **As a** holiday resort, Blackpool Corporation operated a number of trams to cater for those enjoying the summer sun. Prior to the First World War, UEC supplied no fewer than twenty-four single-deck open toastrack cars – No 69-92 on Preston equal-wheel bogies; these were supplemented in 1927 by the purchase of a further six – Nos 161-66 – that were constructed by the corporation on Preston McGuire equal-wheel bogies supplied by either English Electric or Hurst Nelson. All of the toastracks were originally constructed without centre gangways but these were added during 1936 and 1937 with a consequent reduction in seating capacity. No 166 – seen here in Rigby Road depot alongside No 163 (which was used as the basis of the 'Blackpool Belle' illuminated car in 1959) – was, like the surviving toastracks, stored during the Second World War (and threatened with scrapping post-war). It, however, survived alongside No 165, as both were modified in the summer of 1953 to accommodate television equipment used to record the annual illuminations. Surviving in this role until the mid-1960s, No 166 was preserved in 1972 and moved to Crich in June of that year. Restoration to its original 1927 condition was completed two years later. *D.W.K. Jones/National Tramway Museum*

Above: **Completed at** Rigby Road in 1928, Blackpool 'Standard' No 48 incorporated the open-balcony top cover from the original No 48. It was fitted with lower-deck vestibules in September 1931 and was to emerge as fully-enclosed in February 1938. It is seen in this condition at North Pier in late October 1950. The car survived in service until 1962 and was the last tram to operate on the Marton to Royal Oak route when that service was converted to bus operation on 28 October 1962. Preserved, the tram was exported to the Oregon Electric Railway, in the USA, in August 1964. It is still based in Oregon. *Peter N. Williams/Online Transport Archive*

Opposite above: **In 1927,** English Electric supplied Blackpool Corporation with a small four-wheel electric locomotive. It was constructed to haul coal wagons from exchange sidings built adjacent to Copse Road depot in Fleetwood to sidings established at Thornton Gate. This traffic continued until 1949; thereafter the locomotive was used by the Permanent Way Department to haul wagons over the system from its base at Copse Road and it is inside the depot that the locomotive was recorded here in late October 1950 alongside one of the company 'Crossbench' cars that had been converted into a works car. The depot had originally been opened by the Blackpool & Fleetwood Tramroad Co on 14 July 1898; passing to the corporation on 1 January 1920, the building was depot was used largely thereafter as a depot by the Permanent Way Department and for dismantling withdrawn trams. Closed on 27 October 1963, the depot had a number of uses before being finally demolished in 2016. The locomotive was finally withdrawn from service in December 1965 and moved to Crich the following month. It remains in use at the NTM, where it shunts other trams. *Peter N. Williams/ Online Transport Archive*

Opposite below: **The second** of the Gateshead & District single-decks cars constructed during the 1920s to survive is No 5; this was constructed at the company's Sunderland Road Works in 1927 and was fitted with Brill 39E bogies. Seen here outside Newcastle Central station on 14 September 1949, No 5 was sold to BR for use on the Grimsby & Immingham line following the final conversion of the Gateshead system on 4 August 1951 where it became No 20. Withdrawn with the closure of the line on 1 July 1961, No 20 was preserved by the TMS and moved to Crich during 1963. It first operated at the museum on 3 September 1966, whilst work was in progress restoring it to Gateshead & District condition (a process completed in 1973). The car remains in a largely operational – but currently unused – condition at the NTM. *C. Carter*

Above: **When entering** service in Glasgow in November 1928, No 1100 was typical of the 'Kilmarnock Bogies'; however, from October 1929, when it received Brill 61E1 maximum-traction bogies, the car underwent a series of further modifications. These included a further set of replacement bogies, again supplied by the Kilmarnock Engineering Co (but slightly different to those on the production batch) in late 1940, and, most strikingly, being rebuilt in streamlined form during the summer of 1941. In its new guise, No 1100, seen here at Dalmuir West during the summer of 1954, was notionally to survive until September 1962 although it does not seem to have operated in service since November the previous year. Although slated for scrapping, No 1100 somehow survived to be preserved and, when it left Coplawhill in February 1964, it was the last tram – other than those preserved by the corporation – to leave the works. Reaching Crich, the tram operated at the museum for about a decade before being placed on display; since late 2005, it has been stored at Clay Cross. *Phil Tatt/Online Transport Archive*

Opposite: **Following work** on the development of a bogie car, which had involved the rebuilding of 'Standard' No 142 and the construction of a prototype car (No 1090), orders were placed for the construction of fifty new bogie cars during 1928 and 1929; the bodies of these were supplied by Hurst Nelson (Nos 1091-1120), R.Y. Pickering Ltd (Nos 1121-30) and Brush (Nos 1131-40). Although the prototype cars had been fitted with maximum-traction bogies supplied by Hurst Nelson, these fifty cars had bogies produced by the Kilmarnock Engineering Co and so became known as the 'Kilmarnock Bogies'. Unfortunately, the cars were prone to derailing on sharp curves, with the result that they were largely restricted to east-west services such as those to Dalmuir West and Clydebank that were flat and straight. During the war, the seating on the lower deck of all bar three of the type was converted to longitudinal in order to increase the number of standing passengers that could be accommodated. One of the Hurst Nelson-built cars, No 1115 – completed in January 1929 and seen here outside Dalmarnock depot on Ruby Street – was secured for preservation following withdrawal. One of the cars restored to service in March 1961 following the Dalmarnock depot fire, No 1115 was one of last three survivors of the type in service – the others being Nos 1106 and 1133 – when withdrawn for the final time in June 1961. Preserved in December 1962, the car was destined for a site in Cheshire but was diverted en route to Crich where it operated for a period up to 1976. It remains on static display at the museum. *Dr Struan J.T. Robertson/Online Transport Archive*

Above: **During 1928** and 1929, ten single-deck cars – Nos 167-76 – were supplied to Blackpool Corporation by English Electric at the cost of £2,000 each. Fitted with the same supplier's McGuire-type equal-wheel bogies, the trams were delivered with pantographs and so became known as either the 'Pantograph' or 'Pullman' type. The pantographs were all replaced by conventional trolleypoles during 1933. No 167 – seen here at the Fleetwood Ferry terminus in late October 1950 – was converted into a works car in July 1953 and survived in this guise until 1962, when it was replaced by sister car No 170. The tram was donated the TMS and reached Crich in May 1962. The car was transferred to Bolton for restoration in 1983 with work being completed in time for it to return to Blackpool for the centenary of the system in 1985. It has since operated at the Gateshead Garden Festival – in 1988 – at Beamish and made other return trips to its home system. It remains, at the time of writing, one of the NTM's operational fleet. Of the remaining nine cars, six were scrapped but three – Nos 170, 172 and 175 – were used as the basis of new illuminated trams in Blackpool. *Peter N. Williams/Online Transport Archive*

Opposite above: **For the** introduction of electric trams to the Swansea & Mumbles on 2 March 1929, Brush supplied thirteen fully-enclosed double-deck cars; Nos 1-11 arrived in 1928 and the remaining two the following year. All were fitted with Brush equal-wheel bogies and could accommodate 106 seated passengers. This made the trams amongst the largest first-generation trams to operate in Britain. Unusually, the trams were designed with doors on only one side – the landward – and all survived until the route's conversion to bus operation in two stages (on 11 October 1959 and 5 January 1960). Of these, eleven were scrapped soon after closure but No 2 was secured for preservation and moved to the Middleton Railway in Leeds; unfortunately, it suffered from vandalism whilst based there and was subsequently scrapped. The only surviving part of the fleet now on display is one cab section of No 7 – seen here at the Mumbles Bay terminus on 4 September 1955 – which was one of two cars – the other being No 6 – that were specially decorated for the final services. This is now displayed in the National Waterfront Museum in Swansea. *Julian Thompson/Online Transport Archive*

Opposite below: **Between 1925** and 1929, the Dublin United Tramways Co constructed ten fully-enclosed 'Standard Saloons' at its Spa Road Works; these were Nos 181/84, 218/24/52-55/78/84 – with two more being converted from older cars: No 313 rebuilt from a prototype car of 1906 and No 314 being rebuilt from an open-balcony car in 1929. All were fitted with Hurst Nelson bogies with the first two to be completed – Nos 218 and 224 – being initially used on the Dalkey route. However, following the acquisition and conversion of the Lucan route, the cars were allocated to that service – becoming known as 'Lucan Bogies' as a result – until its conversion to bus operation in 1940. No 313 was withdrawn during the Second World War, leaving the remaining eleven cars to operate the Dalkey service until its conversion on 9 July 1949. No 284 – seen here alongside No 44 and works car No 24 – of 1928 was not preserved on withdrawal but its body was subsequently secured for preservation and it is currently under restoration at the National Transport Museum of Ireland into an open-balcony car (a condition in which it never actually operated). The museum also accommodates the restored body – without bogies or seats – of No 253. Used after withdrawal as a classing room and sleeping accommodation at Dun Laoghaire, the body was recovered in 1987 and restored at Broombridge. *F.N.T. Lloyd-Jones/Online Transport Archive*

Above: **During the** early 1920s, Glasgow Corporation, like most tramway operators, was facing unrestricted bus competition and was suffering, as a result, from loss of traffic. During June 1925, work started on the production of a new high-speed single-deck car. When No 1089 emerged from Coplawhill Works in August 1929, it was equipped with two Brill 77E1 bogies and provided accommodation for thirty-six seated passengers. Nicknamed 'Baillie Burt's Car' after the then convenor of the transport committee, Peter Burt, the seating accommodation on the car was not ideal in operation and led to the car's transfer to the Duntocher to Clydebank route in August 1932. Withdrawn following the conversion of this route on 3 December 1949, No 1089 was restored to service, with modified seating, in December 1951 for use on workmen's services to and from John Brown's shipyard. Its operation was much reduced from the summer of 1960 but, following the Dalmarnock depot fire of 22 March 1961, it returned to more regular service until final withdrawal three months later. Stored thereafter, it was used in the final closure procession in September 1962. It is now preserved in the Glasgow Riverside Museum, Here the tram is seen heading at the Whiteinch terminus on Dumbarton Road prior to heading to Partick on 5 August 1959. *Hamish Stevenson/Online Transport Archive*

Opposite: **The evolution** of the 'Feltham' bogie car for the London United Tramways and Metropolitan Electric Tramways saw a number of experimental cars constructed during the 1920s and a final non-standard car – MET No 331 – was built contemporaneously with the construction of the 100 production cars and entered service in late 1930. Built by the Union Construction Co of Feltham, No 331 was fitted a centre-entrance body and equipped with Union Construction Co-built equal-wheel bogies. It entered service in December 1930 and was used initially on route 40 from Whetstone to Cricklewood. Following the creation of the LPTB, the tram was renumbered 2168. However, the policy of the newly-created body – of tram to trolleybus conversion – resulted in the premature withdrawal of No 331 in August 1936 as its unique design precluded the fitting of conduit ploughs – essential for transfer to the largely conduit-powered network south of the river – and, the following year, the car was sold to Sunderland Corporation where, fitted with a pantograph in place of its trolleypoles, it entered service in 1937. Stored, along with a number of other cars during the Second World War, No 100 returned to service post-war but was withdrawn in May 1951. Offered for sale, it was purchased for preservation by the LRTL the following year. The car is seen here outside Hylton Road depot in April 1952. Stored following its removal from Sunderland in a number of locations – including Bradford Corporation's Thornbury Works – No 331 arrived at Crich in June 1961. Restored in the late 1980s initially as Sunderland No 100 – in order to enable it to feature at the 1989 Garden Festival at Gateshead – the car has subsequently been returned to its original guise as MET No 331. *Phil Tatt/Online Transport Archive*

In 1930, the LCC took delivery of a batch of 50 'HR/2' cars – Nos 1854-1903 – that were built by English Electric and fitted with EMB Heavyweight bogies. These cars, as was required at the time by the Metropolitan Police, had open lower-deck vestibules but fully-enclosed upper decks. The following year a further batch of sixty cars – Nos 101-60 – were built by Hurst Nelson; however, No 160, although scheduled to be an 'HR/2', was fitted with 'E/3' type maximum traction bogies when its scheduled EMB bogies were used in the construction of No 1. The 1931-built cars were fitted with lower-deck windscreens from new and, during the 1930s, the original English Electric cars were modified to become fully-enclosed. Four of the batch – Nos 1884, 1885, 1887 and 1890 – passed through the LPTB's Rehabilitation programme in the late 1930s whilst a further three – Nos 1881, 1883 and 1886 – were sold to Leeds Corporation in 1938. A total of 16 cars – Nos 112/23-25/29-31/48 and 1865/89/98-903 – were destroyed during the war with a number of others seriously damaged. Designed for operation on the hilly routes that served Dulwich via the steep four-tracked Dog Kennel Hill – the 56, 58, 60, 62 and 84 – the majority of the then surviving cars were withdrawn when these routes were converted to bus operation as Stage 5 of 'Operation Tramaway' on 6 October 1951. The one surviving 'HR/2' – No 1858 seen here passing the junction with Blackheath Hill with an inbound service on route 58 towards Victoria on 12 August 1951 – was privately preserved in 1952. Having spent more than a decade in the open air at Chessington Zoo, the car was moved to the East Anglian Transport Museum at Carlton Colville in April 1964. It is still based at the museum having been restored to an operational condition. *Julian Thompson/Online Transport Archive*

William Chamberlain was appointed general manager in Belfast in 1929; a strong proponent of tramcar development, he oversaw the reconditioning of much of the existing fleet and the purchase of a batch of fifty new trams – Nos 342-91 – that were delivered in 1930. Known as the 'Chamberlain' class, the first forty were built by Brush with the final ten being completed by the Belfast-based Service Motor Works Ltd. All were fitted by M&T 8ft 0in swing link four-wheel trucks. All were withdrawn between 1951 and 1954 with No 357, which survived in service until the system's final closure, being preserved. The car is seen here entering the short section of single-track line on the final approach to the Ligoniel terminus. All day services on the routes serving Ligoniel ceased on 10/11 October 1953 with the official closure following on 28 February 1954. No 357 is now based at the Ulster Folk and Transport Museum at Cultra. *Marcus Eavis/Online Transport Archive*

Constructed as a rail derrick (or self-propelled tower wagon), Leeds No 2 – pictured here on 8 October 1950 – was constructed at Kirkstall Road Works in 1931 on the Peckham Cantilever four-wheel truck salvaged from withdrawn No 110A. The works car was designed to assist in the construction of reserved track sections that were inaccessible to conventional road-based tower wagons. Initially, the car was fitted with both a conventional trolleypole and bow collector – the condition in which it is now preserved – but, in 1938, the former was replaced by a second bow collector. In December 1953, its original truck was replaced by a second – and similar – truck reused from another works car (No 1 which had previously been No 80A). No 2 was renumbered 1 at the same time and survived in service until the closure of the Leeds system in November 1959. Preserved initially along with trams on the Middleton Railway, it was more fortunate than others based there being transferred, following purchase by the Leeds Transport Historical Society, to a site at Garforth Bridge in January 1964, where restoration work was undertaken, before transfer to Crich in June 1969. It remains in an operational state at the museum. *R.B. Parr/National Tramway Museum*

The Falkirk & District Tramways Co operated a network of just over 7¾ route miles; the 4ft 0in gauge system opened on 21 October 1905 and survived until 21 July 1936. Latterly, the system was operated exclusively by single-deck trams, with the original fleet being replaced between 1929 and 1933 by the purchase of fourteen new single-deck cars from Brush – Nos 1-10 during 1929 and 1930 and Nos 13-16 in 1931 – that were equipped with the same manufacturer's Burnley bogies and four second-hand trams – Nos 11-12 and 17-19 – acquired from Dearne District Light Railways. The body of No 14 – pictured outside the company's depot on Larbert Road, Carmuirs, with sister car No 17 in the background – was sold off after closure and became a garden shed at Slamannan. Rescued for preservation in 1979 on behalf of Falkirk Museums, the tram was restored using Hurst Nelson bogies that had been new for use on the 4ft 0in gauge Glasgow subway. The tram, in its fully restored condition, is stored at the museum's workshop in Grangemouth. *Photo by D.L.G. Hunter, courtesy A.W. Brotchie*

Following a period of experimentation, 100 production 'Feltham' cars were manufactured by the Union Construction Co for the LUT (forty-six cars) and MET (fifty-four); constructed in 1931, the cars were fitted – with one exception – with EMB bogies when new. However, the creation of the LPTB in 1933 and the decision to convert from tram to trolleybus meant that the 'Felthams' spent a relatively short period of time operating the routes for which they were designed before being transferred south of the river. Two of the type were destroyed by enemy action during the Second World War and a number were withdrawn during the early post-war years; this meant that, by the time that the final conversion programme ('Operation Tramaway'') was instituted, some ninety of the type were still operational. Leeds Corporation had been in the market for second-hand trams earlier in the decade and the corporation's rolling stock engineer – Victor Matterface – had come to Leeds from London Transport; he knew the 'Felthams' well and, in October 1949, arranged for one of the batch – No 2099 – to travel to the West Riding on loan for evaluation purposes. It operated in LT livery but with the corporation's crest on the side and retained its original LT number; it is seen here at Belle Isle in this condition on an enthusiasts' tour in June 1950. As a result of the loan, the corporation decide to purchase the remaining cars. A total of ninety arrived in Leeds; a further two – Nos 2144 and 2162 – were destroyed by fire in London. Of the ninety, all of the ex-MET cars entered service as Leeds Nos 501-50 – Nos 2099 had been renumbered 501 in August 1950 – with the ex-LUT cars being renumbered 551-90 (although not all of these entered service). However, a reversal of policy in Leeds led to the conversion of the tram services to bus operation and many of the 'Felthams' had a relatively short life in the West Riding. No 2099 was to survive until the system's final conversion in November 1959 and was transferred to the Museum of British Transport at Clapham the following month. Becoming part of the London Transport Museum and restored as MET No 355 in static condition, the tram is based at the time of writing at the museum's Acton store. *Peter N. Williams/Online Transport Archive*

A second ex-MET 'Feltham' to be preserved is No 341, which became LPTB No 2085 in 1933 and is seen in this condition on Camberwell New Road on 30 September 1950. Like the majority of the ex-MET cars, No 2085 was a relatively early casualty, being withdrawn by the date of this photograph (and so presumably en route to the Tramatorium at Penhall Road when recorded here). It travelled to Leeds three months later and entered service, as No 526 in March 1951. Another of the batch to survive until November 1959, the car was purchased by the Seashore Trolley Museum of Kennebunkport and shipped across the Atlantic in 1960. The car remains at Seashore in an unrestored condition. A third 'Feltham' was also preserved following the closure of the Leeds system; this was one of the ex-LUT cars (LPTB No 2138 that had been Leeds No 554 until renumbered 517 in February 1959). Unfortunately, this car was heavily vandalised whilst stored in the open on the Middleton Railway and subsequently scrapped; fortunately, its bogies survived and were used in the restoration of 'E/1' No 1622 (see page 85). *F.N.T. Lloyd-Jones/Online Transport Archive*

Above: **Following the** construction of the four prototype 'Horsfield' or 'Showboat' cars, Nos 151-54 in Kirkstall Works, Brush supplied Leeds Corporation with a batch of 100 cars – Nos 155-254 – during 1931 and 1932. The first fifty were equipped BTH electrical equipment whilst Nos 205-54 were fitted with equipment supplied by GEC; all were originally equipped with Peckham P35 four-wheel trucks. Along with the 'Felthams', this type of tram was one of the mainstays of the Leeds system during its final years. Following the conversion of the Moortown and Dewsbury Road services on 28 September 1957, thirty of the GEC-equipped cars were withdrawn but the first of the BTH batch withdrawn was No 180 in November 1957; slated for scrapping, No 180 – which was new originally in 1931 and which is pictured here at the Moortown terminus about to head southwards towards the city centre and Dewsbury Road – was reprieved in March 1958 when No 189 was seriously damaged in a collision with a West Yorkshire bus. Nos 180 and 189 exchanged identities, with the original No 189 being scrapped. As such, the new No 189 survived until the system's final closure and was preserved, moving to Crich in January 1960. It remains part of the NTM's operational fleet, having now clocked up more than fifty years of service. Two other 'Horsfields' were also secured for preservation initially. No 160 was sold to the Middleton Railway and transferred in May 1961; however, it suffered serious vandalism and its remains were transferred to the city's Armley Mills Industrial Museum. Deemed beyond economic repair, its remains were scrapped in 1981. Its truck, however, survived and is now under Sunderland No 16 at Beamish. On closure, No 202 was donated to Leeds City Museum; again stored on the Middleton Railway, it suffered serious vandalism as well and its remains were scrapped in January 1964. *Keith Carter/Online Transport Archive*

Opposite: **During 1931** and 1932 a batch of twelve bogie cars – Nos 758-69 – was constructed at Edge Lane Works by Liverpool Corporation; fitted with English Electric equal-wheel bogies, the cars became known as 'English Electric bogies' and their performance helped to change the popular perception of the city's trams and paved the way for the modernisation of the system in the late 1930s under the general manager W.G. Marks. Fitted with comfortable seats, the cars were fast, smooth and airy. Between 1938 and 1944, Nos 759-62/64-67/69 were reconditioned and fitted with new motors, improved destination displays and EMB lightweight bogies that had originally been intended for use under further new 'Liner' cars. The remaining three cars were stored pre-war but not scrapped until 1948. Five of the batch – Nos 760/62/64-66 – survived in service until March 1955. The lower deck of No 762, which is seen in August 1952 on a route 6 service on Roe Street, was transferred to the Parks & Gardens Department for use as a clubhouse at Newsham Park. It was rescued in 1977 and restored to operational condition by the members of the Merseyside Tramway Preservation Society at the Wirral Transport Museum using ex-Blackpool Corporation English Electric 4ft 0in wheelbase bogies. *Phil Tatt/Online Transport Archive*

In June 1932, LCC launched a new double-deck ; No 1, fitted with the EMB Class 6A radial bogies from No 160, was designed as the prototype for a possible new fleet of trams; however, the creation of the LPTB the following year and that body's decision to pursue a policy of replacing tram with trolleybuses, meant that No 1 – which was nicknamed 'Bluebird' when new as a result of its non-standard blue livery – remained a one-off. The car survived in service in London until April 1951. The generally accepted thesis is that No 1 was sold to Leeds Corporation in lieu of two 'Feltham' cars – Nos 2144 and 2162 – that had been destroyed by fire after their sale to Leeds but before their final withdrawal in London. More recently discovered documentation – and I'm grateful to Dave Jones of the LCCTT for the material – suggests that Leeds were offered the salvageable parts from the two 'Felthams' for £500 and, when No 1 was withdraw a few months later, that car was also made available for £500. There would appear to be no mention in the records that it went to Leeds as compensation. In any event, it re-entered service as Leeds No 301 in December 1951 and is pictured here at the Lawnswood terminus in April 1954. Following withdrawal in 1957, it was presented to the Museum of British Transport at Clapham. Transferred to the NTM in 1973, work started on a major restoration project in June 2014 largely funded by the LCCTT; at the time of writing work is approaching completion. *Phil Tatt/Online Transport Archive*

Following the appointment of Walter Luff as general manager and the decision to acquire new trams from English Electric, No 225 was delivered in January 1934. This was an open single-deck car – designated as a 'Luxury Toastrack' but more popularly known as a 'Boat' – fitted with the same manufacturer's 4ft 0in wheelbase bogies. The new trams proved popular with both crews and passengers with the result that a further eleven – Nos 226-36 – were ordered; these were delivered during the summer of 1934. The production cars were identifiable from the original in having slightly higher body sides. Of the twelve cars, four – Nos 229/31/32/34 – were withdrawn and scrapped in the 1960s, leaving the remaining eight – renumbered 600-07 in 1967 – operational. No 601 became the first of the type to cross the Atlantic in 1971, to be followed by No 603 in 1976 to help mark the bicentenary of US independence, but the surviving six soldiered on. By the first decade of this century, the ranks were further thinned, although three – Nos 600, 602 and 604 – remain as part of the Blackpool heritage fleet. No 233 – seen here on 28 June 1967 prior to renumbering as No 605 – was initially preserved by the Lancastrian Transport Trust and was loaned to Beamish for a period. In September 2013, three months before its collection donated to the Blackpool Heritage Trust (the body established to ensure the ongoing preservation of the historic fleet in Blackpool), No 605 was sold to the San Francisco-based Muni Tramway; thus No 605 became the fourth 'Boat' to be preserved across the pond. *Geoffrey Tribe/Online Transport Archive*

Above: Following the construction of prototype car No 1 by the Cravens Railways Carriage & Wagon Co in 1927, a total of 210 standard fully-enclosed cars were constructed for Sheffield Corporation between 1928 and 1935. Of these, 185 were built by the corporation itself at Queen's Road, with the remaining 25 – Nos 131-55 – being constructed by W. & E. Hill Ltd. All were fitted with Peckham P22 four-wheel trucks. A total of ten – Nos 83, 85, 100/12/19/29/33/192, 201/27 – were destroyed by enemy action during the Second World War but the remainder were withdrawn from the early 1950s onwards as the Sheffield system contracted. Delivered in 1934, No 189 – pictured here on an enthusiasts' tour – was originally allocated to Holm Lane depot and subsequently to Tenter Street before withdrawal in April 1958. Presented to the TMS, the car was stored in Tinsley depot for more than two years as the TMS at that stage still had no museum site. As a result, the car was to operate for the last time in its home city as part of the final closure procession on 8 October 1960 before being moved to Crich later the same month. Used in service at the museum between 1969 and 1980, the condition of the car's bodywork currently precludes operation and it remains on static display in the museum. *Barry Cross Collection/Online Transport Archive*

Opposite above: As part of his programme for the modernisation of the Blackpool Corporation fleet, Walter Luff wanted a replacement for the open-top 'Dreadnought' cars – see No 59 (page 50) – and English Electric constructed a prototype 'Luxury Dreadnought' open-top car – No 225 – that entered service in February 1934. Fitted with the same supplier's 4ft 9in bogies, the car was renumbered 237 shortly after entering service. Proving a success, a further twelve open-top cars – Nos 238-249 – were ordered and these entered service between September 1934 and April 1935. All of these open-top cars were fitted with fully enclosed top covers during 1941 and 1942 for wartime service and thus appeared externally identical to the fully-enclosed 'Balloon' cars Nos 250-63. From the late 1950s onwards, the majority of the type received modified single destination blinds – as shown by No 712 (which had been No 249 prior to the 1968 renumbering) as it heads north towards Bispham on 30 May 1970 – and over the long history of the type further modifications were undertaken. No 712, which had undergone a major refurbishment in 1982, was last to operate in Blackpool in November 2009 and, having been repainted into the livery the type had carried in the 1920s, was acquired by the NTM the following year. No 712 is currently on static display at Crich. *Geoffrey Tribe/Online Transport Archive*

Opposite below: Entering service in March 1935, Blackpool No 258 became No 721 when the fleet was renumbered in 1968. The car, which is seen here heading north towards Fleetwood passing the Metropole Hotel in 1995, was finally withdrawn from service in October 2009 and was acquired by the North Eastern Electrical Transport Trust in March 2012. The tram was transferred to NELSAM, where it is still based, in May 2013. *Geoffrey Tribe/Online Transport Archive*

Above: **Following the** closure of the Lytham St Annes system in 1935, Blackpool Corporation needed to supplement its fleet in order to replace the Lytham trams that had exercised running powers south from North Pier. Rather than reorder a batch from English Electric, which had supplied eighty-four streamlined cars between 1933 and 1935, the corporation placed an order for twenty cars with Brush, as William Lockhart Marshall (who had been instrumental in the development of the original trams at English Electric) was now employed by Brush as a consultant. There were some detail differences between the Brush-built cars and those supplied by English Electric as the latter company held a number of patents to the design. Nos 284-303 were delivered during 1937 and all were fitted with EMB hornless equal-wheel bogies. The development of the type over more than seventy years is complex – suffice to note that No 635 – seen here at Bispham on 14 September 1974 – had originally been No 298 when new; when withdrawn later that year, the tram, albeit in a poor state, was secured for preservation as it was deemed to be the closest to its original condition. For some thirty years the tram led a somewhat itinerant life, with limited restoration work being undertaken, before being transferred to Crich in 2005. Being based at Clay Cross since 2014, at the time of writing, work is planned to start to restore the car fully. *Gerald Druce/Online Transport Archive*

Opposite above: **Whilst Blackpool** was constructing modern streamlined trams in the early 1930s, on the Isle of Man, Douglas Corporation was still acquiring new horse trams. In 1935, three new convertible cars – Nos 48-50 – were acquired from the Vulcan Motor & Engineering Co. Modified in the late 1970s, all three were sold to the Manx Electric Railway in 1980 for use as passenger shelters; however, only No 49 – seen here in open crossbench form during the summer of 1956 at Victoria Pier – was used for the purpose with the other two being scrapped. Rescued for preservation in 1982 and initially displayed at the Electric Railway Museum at Ramsey, the tram has been in store since 2011. *Phil Tatt Collection/Online Transport Archive*

Opposite below: **In 1935,** Blackpool Corporation constructed a second railgrinder at Rigby Road; No 2 was fitted with the Brush Flexible four-wheel truck salvaged from a withdrawn car. Entering service on 25 May 1935, the major difference between No 2 and No 1 was that the former had sliding doors on only one side whilst the latter had doors on both sides. The only significant modification to the car during its years of service was the addition of snowploughs in November 1935. With the contraction of the Blackpool system in the early 1960s, the need for railgrinding was significantly reduced with the result that No 2 – seen here inside Blundell Street depot alongside No 1 – was withdrawn in October 1965 and arrived at Crich two months later. Used for a period as a works car and as a mobile generator, No 2 was taken out of service in March 1975 and transferred to the Clay Cross store. It has subsequently been cannibalised for parts to restore other trams; this included, for a period, its truck being used under Chesterfield No 7. It remains in long-term storage in an unrestored condition. *R.W.A. Jones/Online Transport Archive*

The NTM is also home to a second of the Brush-built single-deck cars of 1937; this is No 630 which was No 293 when new in August 1937. Becoming No 630 in 1968, the car is seen at Little Bispham on 29 June 1985, with the then brand-new 'Centenary' class No 641 in the background. The tram carried the overall livery promoting Tussaud's Waxworks that it carried for the three summers from 1985 and until 1987. No 630 underwent a major overhaul in 1996 and was one of only two of the type – the other being No 631 – to escape being stored at the end of the 2004 season (although others were subsequently restored to service). No 630 remained operational until towards the end of the conventional tramway in 2011 but was withdrawn shortly before November of that year, leaving only Nos 631 and 632 operational, and was repainted in the green and cream livery adopted by Blackpool in the 1990s. It departed for Crich on 21 December 2011 and is part of the NTM's operational fleet. It spent the period between September 2017 and May 2018 back in its home town as part of the events to mark the 80th anniversary of the type's introduction to service. *Geoffrey Tribe/Online Transport Archive*

During 1936 and 1937, a total of 163 high-speed streamlined bogie cars were constructed at Liverpool Corporation's Edge Lane Works to a design by R.J. Heathman. Of these, 151-88, 879/81-917/43-52/55/57 were fitted with EMB lightweight bogies, No 918-42 with M&T swing-link bogies and Nos 868-70/80, 953/56/58-92 with EMB heavyweight 'Jo-burg'-style bogies when new. More than twenty of the type were withdrawn by the end of the 1940s, including nineteen destroyed as a result of the Green Lane depot fire of November 1947 but it was not until September 1953 that the first withdrawals not caused by either fire or accident damage occurred. In late 1953 and early 1954, Glasgow Corporation acquired twenty-four of the M&T-equipped cars; this was followed by the purchase, in March 1954, of a further twenty-two cars, this time fitted with either EMB lightweight or heavyweight bogies. Regauged to 4ft 7¾in, the trams became Nos 1006-16/18-38/41-59/52-56 in Scotland. Amongst the second batch to be sold was Liverpool No 869 – seen here alongside 'Baby Grand' No 224 on the south Loop at the Pier Head on 3 April 1954 – which became Glasgow No 1055. It re-entered service on 2 November 1955 and survived until withdrawal in June 1960. Selected by the Liverpool University Public Transport Society and preserved by the Merseyside Tramway Preservation Society, it was transferred initially to the Middleton Railway before being moved to Crich in November 1961. Six years later, it moved to Liverpool for restoration before returning to Crich in October 1979 where work to return it to its original Liverpool condition was completed in January 1993. It remains part of the NTM's operational fleet. *Martin Jenkins/Online Transport Archive*

Above: **Between 1933** and 1937, Brighton Corporation constructed replacement bodies for thirty-one of its existing fleet with the new trams retaining the Brill 21E four-wheel trucks of the trams that they replaced; the Class F, typified by No 52 pictured here at Race Hill, were destined to have a relatively short operational career as the entire 3ft 6in-gauge network, that extended over almost 9½ route miles at its peak, was finally closed on 31 August 1939. The body of No 53, which was new in 1937, and those of two other trams were converted into sheds at the corporation's Lewes Road Works. Subsequently, the body of No 53 was used on a pig farm at Partridge Green. The body was rescued during the 1970s; it is currently under restoration in its home town under the auspices of the Brighton Tram 53 Society, a group established in 2010 to fund and complete the restoration. *D.W.K. Jones/NTM*

Opposite: **Between 1936** and 1939, Sheffield Corporation constructed sixty-seven four-wheel cars in its own workshops on Peckham P22 trucks. Two of the type – Nos 261 and 274 – were destroyed as a result of enemy action during the Second World War whilst fourteen cars to a similar – but slightly modified – design were constructed between 1941 and 1944 to replace cars destroyed during the war. No 264 – seen here – was new in 1937 and suffered minor wartime damage but was repaired. It survived in normal passenger service until the final conversion of the Sheffield system on 8 October 1960. Not initially selected for preservation, it was privately acquired and transferred to the then relatively new museum site at Crich in December 1960. Restored to operational condition over the next decade, it ran in public service at the museum until 1980 and, since then, has been on display. *Hamish Stevenson/Online Transport Archive*

Above: In the early 1930s, Glasgow Corporation was faced by increasing levels of traffic and thus the necessity of increasing the fleet. The last new cars had been the 'Kilmarnock Bogies', delivered in 1929 and other work had seen the modernisation of the 'Standard' cars. In 1936, two streamlined experimental bogie cars – Nos 1141 and 1142 – were completed and this led to the production of 150 'Coronation' cars – No 1143-292 – between December 1936 and July 1941. All were completed at Coplawhill on EMB lightweight bogies. The latter were fitted with rubber shock absorbers, that improved the ride, whilst the design incorporated platform doors, leather seats, enclosed cabs for the drivers and heating. No 1173 – seen here on 9 July 1954 heading to Auchenshuggle with a service on route 9 with 'Standard' No 657 in pursuit – was new in May 1938. It was one of the trams slightly damaged in the Newlands depot fire of 11 April 1948 but was repaired and returned to service. Withdrawn in February 1962, the car was restored to its original 1938 condition and is the oldest 'Coronation' car to survive. Having been displayed as a static exhibit at a number of local museums, it has been based at the city's Riverside Museum since 2012. *R.J.S. Wiseman*

Opposite above: Known as 'Baby Grands', a total of 100 four-wheel streamlined cars – Nos 201-300 – were constructed by Liverpool Corporation at its Edge Lane Works between 1937 and October 1942 on EMB flexible axle 9ft 0in-wheel base trucks. Some 25 per cent lighter than the similar bogie cars, the four-wheel cars could still accommodate seventy seated passengers. One of the batch was lost to enemy action during the war with a further five being destroyed by fire by the end of 1945. Ten of the type were destroyed as a result of the Green lane depot fire of 7 November 1947, which started as a result of a fire on No 295. With many of the cars in a poor condition by the end of the decade, the corporation undertook a major refurbishment programme between 1950 and 1952, and it was not until September 1956, as Liverpool's conversion programme drew towards its conclusion, that further cars were withdrawn. Some thirty of the type remained operational on the final day – 14 September 1957. No 245, now owned by National Museums Merseyside and on loan to the Wirral Transport Museum (where it was restored to operational condition, re-entering service in September 2015), was new originally in 1938 and was withdrawn in September 1957. It is seen here ascending Mount Vernon in August 1953 with a service on route 6A towards Bowring Park. *Phil Tatt/Online Transport Archive*

Opposite below: A second 'Baby Grand' to survive is No 293, which was completed in 1939; it is seen here on route 6A. This car was selected to be Liverpool's official last tram, for which purpose it was repainted in a reversed predominantly white livery and was withdrawn following the closure ceremony on 14 September 1957. Acquired for preservation by the Seashore Trolley Museum of Kennebunkport, it left its home city on board the *American Packer* on 7 May 1958. It reached its new home, where it remains awaiting restoration, on 23 May 1958. *R.F. Mack/Simon Fozard Collection*

Above: **A second** preserved 'Coronation' car now based in Scotland is June 1939-built No 1245. Seen here outside the Commercial Union Assurance Building (which was designed by John Burnet, Son & Dick and opened in the late 1920s) on St Vincent Street awaiting departure with a service on route 23 – a service that linked Maryhill with Baillieston (which was converted to bus operation on 6 November 1960) – No 1245 was withdrawn in June 1962. Preserved in the open at Measham and subsequently at the East Anglian Transport Museum at Carlton Colville, although not operated (as a result of the difference gauge – Glasgow's 4ft 7¾in as opposed to the standard gauge used at the museum) – No 1245 was transferred to the Summerlee Museum at Coatbridge in 2003 after it had spent five years in store at Blackpool. It is currently undergoing a full restoration, with work on the project having commenced in 2011. *George Fairley Collection/Online Transport Archive*

Opposite above: **Two generations** of Blackpool tram stand outside Marton depot in August 1952. On the left is 'Standard' No 42 whilst on the right is Marton 'VAMBAC' No 11. The former, which was new in 1926 was approaching the end of its career when recorded here – it was withdrawn in 1953 and scrapped five years later – whilst No 11 had only just entered the second phase of its career. Delivered in 1939 as one of a batch of twelve 'Sun Saloons' – Nos 10-21 – that represented the final phase in the development of Blackpool's pre-war streamlined fleet, No 11 – like the other cars of the batch – was rebuilt as fully enclosed during the Second World War. After the war and following the experimental fitting of VAMBAC control to two earlier streamlined cars, the whole batch was modified for use on the Marton route. However, this route was destined to be converted to bus operation in October 1962 and all of the batch bar No 11 were scrapped. No 11 survived initially as its use on a tour in early 1963 had been sought. Preserved at first by the proponents of a scheme to convert the closed Hayling Island branch – closed on 4 November 1963 – into a tramway, the failure of the scheme saw No 11 relocate once again, this time to the East Anglian Transport Museum at Carlton Colville in 1969 where it has been restored to operational condition. *Phil Tatt/Online Transport Archive*

Opposite below: **'Coronation' car** No 1274 was new in January 1940; like the other cars of the type, it was completed at Coplawhill Works on EMB bogies. Pictured here, the car was withdrawn in April 1962 and acquired for preservation by the Seashore Trolley Museum at Kennebunkport in the USA. The car was despatched for its transatlantic trip, along with a spare bogie (from No 1262), on 11 September 1963. The tram was regauged from Glasgow's 4ft 7¾ in gauge to standard gauge for operation and restored to its post-1957 condition. The tram remains at Seashore where it again requires some restoration work. *Martin Jenkins/Online Transport Archive*

A second 'Coronation' car built in 1940 to survive into preservation is No 1282, which is pictured here outside Elderslie Road depot on a particularly wet day. No 1282, which survived until the final closure of the system, was one of the class used in the procession on 4 September 1962; two days later it became the last tram to operate on the system when it made a final journey in Clydebank. Preserved thereafter, it was moved to Crich in March 1963. Restored to an operational condition during 1977 and 1978, it spent twenty-five years as an operational tram at the museum and has been on display, in a non-operational state, since 2003. *Ian G.M. Stewart Collection/Online Transport Archive*

In 1943, Sheffield Corporation acquired ten open-balcony four-wheel cars from Bradford Corporation in order to replace trams that had been destroyed or damaged by enemy action during the war. These cars, all of which were fitted with Brill 21E four-wheel trucks, were regauged from 4ft 0in to standard gauge and fitted with enclosed balconies before re-entering service as Nos 325-34. With the delivery of the new 'Roberts' cars during 1950 and 1951, the ex-Bradford cars were all withdrawn and scrapped with the exception of No 330, which was cut down to single-deck form and utilised as a works car; in such guise, it survived through until the system's final closure in October 1960. Here, No 330, which had originally been Bradford No 251 when built by English Electric in 1920, is seen at Lady's Bridge. *R.W.A. Jones/Online Transport Archive*

Above: **Edinburgh, with** its significant cable tramway, was a relatively late entrant into the operators of electric tramcars. It was only after the Corporation took over the services operated by the Edinburgh & District Co on 30 June 1919 that the existing small electric system – the first electric trams had operated on 8 June 1910 – that the process of conversion commenced. Initially, many of the 'new' electric tramcars were, in fact, converted cable cars but, from the early 1920s, the corporation started to construct new trams, many of which took the numbers of the rebuilt cable cars that they replaced. In 1932, the corporation constructed an experimental car – No 180 – at Shrubhill Works and this was to form the basis of a new class – the 'Shrubhill (or Domed Roof) Standard' – constructed between 1934 and 1950. These were built at Shrubhill on underframes supplied by Hurst Nelson and fitted with Peckham P22 four-wheel trucks. No 35 – seen here whilst on a route 1 service to Fairmilehead passing sister car No 217 on route 9 to Granton – was new in 1948. At this stage, there were no definite plans for the conversion of the Edinburgh system; however, this was to change in 1950 with proposals to convert 25 per cent of the network to bus operation. Two years later complete abandonment became official policy and the last trams operated on 16 November 1956. There were plans to preserve No 225 – the last tram to be completed at Shrubhill – but this car was seriously damaged in an accident shortly before closure and so No 35 was selected in its place. Displayed at a museum located within the works at Shrubhill until closure in 1979, No 35 was transferred to Blackpool in November 1985 where it operated alongside other preserved trams as that system celebrated its centenary. Returning to Scotland in 1988, the car was used at the Glasgow Garden Festival before transfer to Crich in October of that year. The NTM took formal ownership of the car in 2008, the tram is now on static display in the museum. *Ian L. Wright/Online Transport Archive*

Opposite above: **Before the** Second World War, Glasgow Corporation had constructed 150 'Coronation' type double-deck bogie cars; the corporation also had experience of operating the five experimental four-wheel cars – Nos 1001-4/6 – and the unique single-ended car No 1005. Thus, when looking to build new trams after the war, there was considerable knowledge of the strengths and weaknesses of the various options. In the event, the decision was made to purchase a further 100 bogie cars; these became the Mark II 'Coronation' class or the 'Cunarders'. The first of the type – No 1293 – entered service on 1 December 1948 with the last – No 1392 – finally emerging in February 1952. All were fitted with M&T Type 596 bogies. No 1297 – seen here at Millerston on 23 March 1949 when virtually brand-new (it had entered service two months earlier) – was one of the type to service through until the final closure of the system in September 1962. Transferred to Crich in July 1963, the tram has subsequently travelled to Blackpool, for that system's centenary in 1985, and returned to its home city in 1988 when it was one of the cars loaned for operation at the 1988 Garden Festival. *Michael H. Waller*

The last design of traditional four-wheel double-deck tramcar to emerge in Britain was manufactured for Sheffield Corporation by the Horbury-based Charles Roberts & Co Ltd. Nos 502-36 were based upon the earlier corporation-built No 501 – although differing in construction methods and with minor detailing variations – that had emerged in 1946. Fitted with M&T Hornless Type 588 trucks, the trams were delivered between 1950 and 1952. Unfortunately, on 4 April 1951, a report advocating conversion to bus operation was accepted with the result that the new trams only had a relatively short operational life. All survived into the last year of tramway operation – 1960 – and two of the cars were selected to receive special liveries to mark the history of the tramways for the final closure on 8 October 1960. One of the duo was No 510 – seen here at Meadowhead on 7 September 1959 – which was donated to the TMS following the final closure and arrived at Crich in late 1960. Operational when received, the car has been a regular performer, retaining its commemorative livery, at the NTM and remains part of the museum's operational fleet. *Ian Dunnet/ Online Transport Archive*

Above: **The two** Sheffield cars – Nos 510 and 513 – in their special livery in October 1960 seen alongside a third member of the class in normal fleet livery. The three trams are pictured on Angel Street outside the Cockaynes department store. The company's original shop was destroyed during the Sheffield Blitz of December 1940 with the new shop being constructed between 1949 and 1955 and so was comparatively new when recorded here. The shop – later known as Schofields – closed in 1982. No 510 has retained its decorative livery in preservation but No 513 has been restored to the plain livery carried by the third car in the background. *Harry Haddrill/Online Transport Archive*

Opposite: **The second** of the Roberts-built cars from 1950 that Sheffield decorated for the closure of the system in October 1960 was No 513, which is seen here at Vulcan Road awaiting departure with a service to Beauchief. Vulcan Road at Tinsley had been, until the conversion of the Rotherham system in 1949, on the through route linking Sheffield with Rotherham; thereafter it was a terminus serving the heavy industries in the Tinsley area. The Vulcan Road to Beauchief and Millhouses routes were the last to operate in the city. Following the closure ceremony, No 513 was preserved. Stored initially at the Middleton Railway, fortunately escaping the fate of many other trams preserved there, the tram was transferred to the ex-Great Northern Railway goods shed at Cullingworth in September 1962. Stored subsequently in the open at, inter alia, the Keighley & Worth Valley Railway, it was eventually moved to Beamish in 1976 and restored to an operational condition. Unlike No 510, however, the restored car has lost its decorated side panels. Since 2011, No 513 has been based at the East Anglian Transport Museum at Carlton Colville. *J. Joyce/Online Transport Archive*

Above: **The last** of the 'Cunarder' class to be constructed, No 1392 appeared in early 1952, almost three months after the completion of the penultimate car in the batch. The final five cars completed – Nos 1388-92 – were all delayed as a result of problems in the supply of certain components. No 1392 – the last wholly new double-deck tram to be constructed in Britain – is seen here at Central station on 2 July 1959. Following withdrawal following the final closure on 4 September 1962, the tram was displayed for ten years at the Museum of British Transport at Clapham prior to returning to its home city for display initially in the museum established at Coplawhill and subsequently at Kelvin Hall. The tram is now one of those on display in the city's Riverside Museum. *Hamish Stevenson/Online Transport Archive*

Opposite: **Arguably the** most modern of Britain's first generation tramcars, Leeds No 602 was constructed as a prototype for a possible fleet of single-deck cars designed to operate over the subways proposed at the time to replace much of the trackwork in the city centre. Designed in the light of European experience in the operation of US-style Presidents' Conference Committee cars under the control of the corporation general manager, A.B. Findlay (who had arrived from Glasgow in 1949), No 602 was constructed by the locally-based Charles H. Roe, the company that also constructed No 601. Work started on the tram's construction in November 1951, but work was not finished until 16 February 1953, with No 602 entering service on 1 June 1953. The tram was fitted with M&T HS44 Type 717 bogies along with Crompton Parkinson VAMBAC equipment. The tram entered service in a purple – rather than red – and cream livery in honour of the coronation. However, a change of political control resulted in the planned subway scheme being abandoned in favour of conversion to bus operation with the result that No 602, along with Nos 600 and 601 (which was also initially preserved but which suffered vandalism on the Middleton Railway and was subsequently scrapped), were effectively white elephants that eked out their operational careers on the short route 25 from Swinegate to Hunslet. As the conversion scheme progressed, the three single-decks cars were deemed non-standard and so were withdrawn relatively early – on 28 September 1957 – and stored. Secured for preservation following the closure of the Leeds system in November 1959, No 602 moved to Crich in May 1960. Although it has operated occasionally, No 602 is now conserved – as Britain's first all electric tram – on display and is unlikely to be restored to an operational condition. The car is seen here in City Square during April 1954. *Phil Tatt/Online Transport Archive*

Above: **Although Leeds** No 602 was the most modern of the trio of single-deck cars to enter service with the corporation, it was not the last 'new' tram for the operator. That honour fell to No 600, which finally entered service in August 1954. The origins of this rebuilt car lay in Sunderland No 85, which had been built by Brush on the same supplier's maximum traction bogies, that entered service on the Villette Road route in 1931. Stored on Wearside at the start of war in September 1939, it was sold to Leeds for £375 in October 1944. Undergoing some years of testing and modification as Leeds No 288, the prolonged programme to rebuild it as No 600 commenced in late 1948. The tram initially emerged from Kirkstall Works in February 1953 to undergo initial trials but was then to remain unused for a year until further testing was undertaken. The car, with its new EMB Radial Arm Type 6A bogies, was finally completed in July 1954; by this date, however, the once ambitious plans for tram subways had been abandoned and, like the other two cars, No 600 operated the short route to Hunslet, where the car is seen here on 16 September 1954. Withdrawn in September 1957 and stored, No 600 was privately preserved initially and transferred to Crich in May 1960. In 1969, it became the first ex-Leeds tram to operate at the Museum but hasn't run in service since 1972 and is at the time of writing stored away from Crich. *Julian Thompson/Online Transport Archive*

Opposite: **The last** new trams delivered to Blackpool Corporation during Walter Luff's tenure as general manager were twenty-five single-deck bogie cars – Nos 304-28 – supplied by Charles Roberts during 1952 and 1953. Inevitably known as the 'Coronation' class, these cars were fitted with M&T HS44 equal-wheel bogies and Compton-Parkinson VAMBAC equipment. Unfortunately, unlike the streamlined cars that Luff had acquired during the 1930s, these new cars were problematic. Their increased width – 7ft 11in – precluded them from operation on certain sections, although not the main Fleetwood to Starr Gate service that was their primary duty, and there were also issues with axles being prone to failure as well as operational problems with their control equipment causing section breakers to blow. One of the batch – No 313 – was withdrawn in 1963 and used as a source of spare parts and a number of the other cars had their original control equipment replaced by conventional English Electric Z4 controllers salvaged from withdrawn 'Railcoaches'. The last of the VAMBAC-fitted cars were withdrawn by October 1970; one of these – No 304 – survives as part of the Blackpool heritage fleet. The final Z4-fitted car – No 660 (ex-No 324) – was retained by the corporation following withdrawal; it now forms part of the heritage fleet. A second Z4-fitted car – No 663 (seen here in its original guise of No 327 shorn of much of the chrome fittings heading north towards the Tower) – was also preserved. This car has led a somewhat precarious life in preservation, being based for some time at the ill-fated Transperience (West Yorkshire Transport Museum) and the St Helens Transport Museum before returning to its home town in April 2003. It underwent a full restoration in 2018 and is also now part of the heritage fleet. *F.E.J. Ward/Online Transport Archive*

In the late 1960s and early 1970s, as almost forty years earlier, the tramways in Blackpool were at a crossroads; the town routes had been converted to bus operation in the early 1960s, leaving the long Promenade route – from Starr Gate to Fleetwood – operational but the costs of operating this service were making it increasingly uneconomic. In the late 1960s, a number of cars were modified to test their suitability for OMO use. This work led to the decision to rebuild a number of the English Electric 'Railcoaches' and, between October 1972 and June 1976, thirteen OMO cars were so rebuilt. The work included the extension at both ends to accommodate platform doors and the ticket-issuing equipment as well as the introduction of bus-style seating. The extension to the underframes to accommodate the longer platforms proved to be the type's Achilles' heel as the lengthened bodies became prone to sagging and it was planned that the type be replaced by the new 'Centenary' class introduced in 1985. These arrivals resulted in the first withdrawals of the OMO cars in the spring of 1985, but problems with the newer cars meant that a number of OMO cars had longer lives than anticipated. One of the last survivors was No 5 – seen here at Bispham on 14 September 1974 in its original plum and yellow livery – which was withdrawn in March 1993. This car had originally been No 221 when delivered in February 1934; it was used as a works car – No 5 – from 1965 until withdrawn for conversion into an OMO car in October 1971, re-entering service the following year. Stored following withdrawal in 1993, the tram was donated to the NTM in 2000; it is currently in store in an unrestored condition. Sister car No 8 remains in Blackpool as part of the operator's heritage fleet, although it has not been in service since 2010. *Gerald Druce/Online Transport Archive*

Following the trial conversion of Nos 275 and 276 at Blackpool into power car and trailer, the corporation decided to purchase ten new trailers – originally Nos T1-T10 (and, from 1968, Nos 681-90) – and rebuild a further eight of the English-Electric-built Series 2 'Railcoaches'. Nos 271-4 and 277-80 were rebuilt in a style similar to Nos 275 and 276, whilst Metropolitan Cammell-Weymann supplied ten unpowered trailers on M&T Type 796 bogies. As a result of operational experience, seven of twin-sets were modified to operate permanently linked; these were No 271-77 and T1-T7 respectively. The remaining three trailers – by now numbered 688-90 – were early casualties, although their power cars – Nos 678-80 – remained in service. No 274, which become No 674 under the 1968 renumbering, was originally built by English Electric on the same supplier's 4ft 0in equal-wheel bogies in 1935. Nos 674 and 684 – seen here at North Pier with 'Boat' No 605 in the distance on 6 August 1994 – were withdrawn in 2008. Preserved by the North Eastern Electrical Transport Trust in July 2012, the pair were initially stored in Sunderland before transfer to NELSAM, where they remain, in July the following year. *John Meredith/Online Transport Archive*

Above: **Following on** from the conversion of the thirteen single-deck OMO cars, attention turned to two of the 'Balloon' class that had been in store since 1971. No 725, which had been delivered as No 262 in February 1935, was rebuilt in Rigby Road. Authorisation was given in November 1975 for the conversion work and, with the assistance of Metal Sections Ltd, the tram's body was substantially rebuilt; this included lengthened and strengthened underframes, single entrances at the front of the tram and relocated staircases. Replacement 5ft 6in wheelbase bogies – constructed by the corporation – were also fitted as was Brush chopper control. The new car, renumbered 761, was launched on 4 June 1979 and is seen here heading northbound in 1982 with a service towards Cabin. Withdrawn at the end of 2011, No 761 was preserved and remains in Blackpool as part of the Blackpool Heritage Trust fleet having returned from outside storage Fleetwood to Rigby Road on December 2013. *Geoffrey Tribe/Online Transport Archive*

Opposite above: **The second** rebuilt double-deck car, No 762, seen here approaching the Fleetwood terminus in 1998, was rebuilt from No 714; this had originally been No 251 and new in December 1934. Completed in a style largely similar to that of No 761 but retaining the central doors in order to improve passenger flow, No 762 entered service following inspection by the Department of Transport on 27 May 1982. It and No 761 were known as 'Jubilee' cars in honour of the Queen's Silver Jubilee in 1977. During the winter months, both cars operated as OMO cars, when traffic was at a lower level, but during the busier summer months a conductor was also employed. In 2008, No 762 was named after Stuart Pillar, who had designed the two and who had died in 2003. Also withdrawn in early November 2011, No 762 moved to Crich later that month. Following workshop attention, No 762 entered the NTM's operational fleet in 2014. *Geoffrey Tribe/Online Transport Archive*

Opposite below: **Although the** Blackpool OMO cars had served their purpose in reducing the operating costs of the tramway, by the early 1980s, they were starting to evince problems and the corporation decided to replace them. Tenders were put out for the work and East Lancashire Coachbuilders – a company that had not previously been involved in tramcar construction – won the contract to build the bodies. Although twelve cars were planned, in the event only seven were delivered – Nos 641-47 – all of which were fitted with corporation-built 5ft 6in bogies with Metalastik suspension. The first of the cars – seen here at Little Bispham on 29 June 1985 – was delivered in the year that marked the centenary of the tramway and so the type became known as the 'Centenary' class. Seating fifty-four and with up to sixteen standing passengers, the trams were equipped with Thyristor control equipment. Not wholly successful in service, from 1999 onwards the cars underwent modification; this included enlarged destination boxes and modified roofs. No 641 was the second car to be refurbished – in 2000 – and survived in service until withdrawal in July 2011. Preserved by the Fleetwood Heritage Leisure Trust, No 641 spent some years on open display at Pleasure Beach before being relocated to Fleetwood Docks during the summer of June 2019. Of the other six, only one – No 646 – has been scrapped with Nos 642 and 645 part of the heritage fleet, No 643 in use at a school in the Midlands, No 644 on display at Famers Parrs and No 647 at NELSAM, Sunderland. *Geoffrey Tribe/Online Transport Archive*

Above: **In addition** to the seven 'Centenary' cars that East Lancashire Coachbuilders constructed, an eighth body was also built. This became Blackpool No 651 and was an experimental tram for GEC. Fitted with modified M&T HS44 bogies reused from a withdrawn 'Coronation' car, No 651 was fitted with experimental switched reluctance traction motors; this nineteenth century technology had not proved practical until suitable control equipment was developed. Following inspection by the Railway Inspectorate on 21 June 1985, the car entered service on 16 July 1985. In 1990, the car was modified to make it compatible with the original seven 'Centenary' cars and renumbered 648; it is in this guise that the tram was recorded at the Tower on 6 August 1994. Withdrawn in November 2011, plans to preserve the car at Crich fell through with the result that No 648 was retained in Blackpool as part of the heritage fleet. *John Meredith/Online Transport Archive*

Opposite above: **In 1987,** Blackpool Corporation took one of the OMO cars – No 7 – which had been withdrawn that year and transferred it to Mode Wheel Workshops. The plan was to rebuild the car to replicate one of the 'Crossbench' cars that had been built by the Blackpool & Fleetwood Tramroad Co. When it reappeared as No 619 – reclaiming the fleet number that the tram has used in a previous guise (as a Series 2 'Railcoach' from 1968; the car had originally been built at No 282 in 1935) – the tram featured open sides with Perspex sheeting (to prevent draughts and to ensure that passengers did not attempt entry and exit other than through the end platforms) and retained its pantograph. It is in this phase of the tram's story that No 619 is seen at Central Pier on 6 August 1984. In the late 1980s, the Perspex was replaced by wrought iron railings and the car survived like this until withdrawal in 2004; briefly reinstated during 2008 and 2009, the car headed to Heaton Park in exchange for Manchester 765 as part of the 125th anniversary celebrations in 2010. Whilst No 765 subsequently returned to Heaton Park, No 619 has not as yet made the return journey and remains operational at Heaton Park. *John Meredith/Online Transport Archive*

Opposite below: **It seems** strange to be recording examples of trams operated by Britain's second generation tramways in a book on preserved trams but both Manchester Metrolink and West Midlands Metro have now fully replaced their original fleets. For the opening of the former system on 6 April 1992, the Italian-based manufacturer AnsaldoBreda supplied twenty-six T-68 articulated high-floor single-deck trams – Nos 1001-26 – with a further six modified cars – the T-68A (Nos 2001-06) – in 1999 for the Eccles extension. In 2008, the thirty-two cars underwent a refurbishment programme; however, the reliability of the newer Bombardier-built M5000 cars meant that the T-68s and T-68As were withdrawn between 2012 and 2014. Two of the type – Nos 1007 and 1023 – were preserved by the Manchester Transport Museum Society with a view to operation eventually at Heaton Park; at the time of writing, No 1007 remains in Manchester whilst No 1023 has been transferred for temporary display at the Crewe Heritage Centre. In addition to these two, the bodyshell of single-car prototype No 1000, which was built to promote the new system in 1990, is preserved at the Greater Manchester Museum of Transport in Boyle Street depot. Here No 1023 is pictured departing Shudehill towards Manchester Victoria station on 17 May 2003. *Geoffrey Tribe/Online Transport Archive*

AnsaldoBreda also supplied the initial fleet for the Midland Metro when the line from Birmingham to Wolverhampton opened on 30 May 1999. Designated T-69 the 16 articulated trams – Nos 01-16 – were constructed between 1996 and 1999. Unlike trams supplied to Manchester Metrolink, the West Midlands Metro examples were low floor. The replacement Spanish-built Urbos 3 trams entered service from September 2014 onwards, and the last of the T-69s were withdrawn in August 2015. Initially all bar No 16 – retained by the operator – were sent to Long Marston for storage (where No 16 was eventually sent as well) with a view to further usage elsewhere. These plans came to nought and in early 2018, the majority of the T-69s were sold for scrap. However, Nos 07 (donated to UK Trams) and 11 (preserved by the City of Birmingham) were preserved whilst Nos 10 and 16 remain in store at Long Marston at the time of writing. In this view, No 7 (which was later to be named *Billy Wright* after the Wolves and England footballer) is seen heading towards Wolverhampton St George's as it departs from The Royal stop in 1999, shortly after the system opened. *Geoffrey tribe/Online Transport Archive*

BIBLIOGRAPHY

Anderson, R.C.; *The Tramways of East Anglia*; LRTL; 1969

Bett, W.H., and Gillham, J.C, edited by Price, J. H.; *The Tramways of Eastern Scotland*; LRTA; undated

Bett, W.H., and Gillham, J.C, edited by Price, J.H.; *The Tramways of North Lancashire*; LRTA; undated

Bett, W.H., and Gillham, J.C, edited by Price, J.H.; *The Tramways of North-East England*; LRTL; undated

Bett, W.H., and Gillham, J.C, edited by Price, J.H.; *The Tramways of South Wales*; LRTA; undated

Bett, W.H., and Gillham, J.C, edited by Price, J.H.; *The Tramways of South West England*; LRTA; undated

Bett, W.H., and Gillham, J.C, edited by Price, J.H.; *The Tramways of South-East Lancashire*; LRTL; undated

Bett, W.H., and Gillham, J.C, edited by Price, J.H.; *The Tramways of the East Midlands*; LRTL; undated

Bett, W.H., and Gillham, J.C, edited by Price, J.H.; *The Tramways of the South Midlands*; LRTA; undated

Bett, W.H., and Gillham, J.C, edited by Price, J.H.; *The Tramways of Yorkshire and Humberside*; LRTA; undated

Bett, W.H., and Gillham, J.C, edited by Wiseman, R.J.S.; *The Tramways of the West Midlands*; LRTA; undated

Brotchie, Alan,; *Scottish Tramway Fleets*; NB Traction; 1968

Brotchie, Alan; *Lanarkshire's Trams*; NB Traction; 1993

Coakham, Desmond; *Tramway Memories: Belfast*; Ian Allan Publishing; 2005

Gandy, Kenneth; *Sheffield Corporation Tramways*; Sheffield City Libraries; 1985

Gillham, J.C, and Wiseman, R.J.S.; *The Tramways of South Lancashire and North Wales*; LRTA; undated

Gillham, J.C, and Wiseman, R.J.S.; *The Tramways of the South Coast*; LRTA; undated

Gillham, J.C, and Wiseman, R.J.S.; *The Tramways of West Yorkshire*; LRTA; undated

Gillham, J.C, and Wiseman, R.J.S.; *The Tramways of Western Scotland*; LRTA; undated

Hearse, George S.; *The Tramways of Northumberland*; Author; 1961

Kilroy, James; *Irish Trams*; Colourpoint Press; 1996

King, J.S.; *Bradford Corporation Tramways*; Venture Publications; 1998

Marshall, Maurice; *Stockport Corporation Tramways*; Manchester Transport Museum Society; 1975

Maybin, J.M.; *Belfast Corporation Tramways 1905-1954*; LRTL; undated

Maybin, Mike; *A Nostalgic Look at Belfast Trams since 1945*; Silver Link; 1994

Smeeton, C.S.; *The London United Tramways: Volume 1 – Origins to 1912*; LRTA & TLRS; 1994

Smeeton, C. .; *The London United Tramways: Volume 2 – 1933 to 1933*; LRTA & TLRS; 2000

Soper, J.; Leeds Transport: Volume 2 – 1902-1931; Leeds Transport Historical Society; 1996

Soper, J.; Leeds Transport: Volume 3 – 1932-1953; Leeds Transport Historical Society; 2003

Soper, J.; Leeds Transport: Volume 4 – 1953-1974; Leeds Transport Historical Society; 2007

Staddon, S.A.; *The Tramways of Sunderland*; Advertiser Press; 1964

Stewart, Ian; *The Glasgow Tramcar*; Scottish Tramway Museum Society; 1983

Taylor, C.; *Manchester's Transport – Part 1: Tramway & Trolleybus Rolling Stock*; Manchester Transport Historical Collection; 1965

Waller, Michael H., and Waller, Peter; *British & Irish Tramway Systems since 1945*; Ian Allan Publishing; 1992

Waller, Peter; *Regional Tramways: London*; Pen & Sword; 2019

Waller, Peter; *Regional Tramways: Midlands & Southern England*; Pen & Sword; 2018

Waller, Peter; *Regional Tramways: Scotland*; Pen & Sword; 2016

Waller, Peter; *Regional Tramways: The North-West England post 1945*; Pen & Sword; 2017

Waller, Peter; *Regional Tramways: Wales, Isle of Man & Ireland post 1945*; Pen & Sword; 2017

Waller, Peter; *Regional Tramways: Yorkshire & North East of England*; Pen & Sword; 2016

Waller, Peter; *The Classic Trams*; Ian Allan Ltd; 1993

Willoughby, D.W., and Oakley, E. R.; *London Transport Tramways Handbook*; Authors; 1972